WHAT DOES IT MEAN TO BE HUMAN?

WHAT DOES IT MEAN TO BE HUMAN?

Reverence for Life Reaffirmed by Responses from Around the World

Compiled and Edited by
FREDERICK FRANCK,
JANIS ROZE, and RICHARD CONNOLLY

St. Martin's Griffin
New York

This book is the result of many years of gathering that would have been unthinkable without the warm cooperation of those who responded to the question: What does it mean to be human? To all of them we are extremely grateful. Their responses have convinced us that we can consider this book, the result of a chain reaction of commitment, as one phase of a project that will include more books, audio- and video-tapes and films, as well as digital programs designed for people of all ages.

Library of Congress Cataloging-in-Publication Data

What does it mean to be human? : reverence for life reaffirmed by responses from around the world / [edited by] Frederick Franck, Janis Roze, and Richard Connolly.
　　　　p. cm.
　　ISBN 0-312-27237-4 (hc)
　　ISBN 0-312-27101-8 (pbk)
　　1. Philosophical anthropology. 2. Man (Theology) I. Franck, Frederick, 1909– II. Roze, Janis A., 1926– III. Connolly, Richard.
　BD450. W4872 2000
　179.7—dc21　　　　　　　　　　　　　　　　　00-027842

First St. Martin's Griffin Edition: November 2001

10　9　8　7　6　5　4　3　2

Contents

The image of the cosmos as a bamboo grove

suggests the intricate possibilities of roots

and branches, strength and flexibility,

growth and development, large and small . . .

Seen in the context of a bamboo grove,

responses to the question

"What does it mean to be human?"

suggest the intricate possibilities

of being human.

WHAT DOES IT MEAN TO BE HUMAN?

Prologue

Frederick Franck

Born on the Dutch-Belgian border, I was five years old when, on August 4, 1914, the twentieth century began in earnest. The Kaiser's armies invaded Belgium half a mile from our doorstep. The First World War had started. The big German field guns were booming all too close by and almost at once an endless stream of wounded and dying soldiers on improvised ambulances, pushcarts, horse-drawn wagons crossed the border into neutral Holland. Endless files of wretched people fleeing their burning villages passed my window, children and belongings on their backs—advance guard of the millions who would trudge from border to border all through the tragic century I happened to survive almost from beginning to end.

I not only survived it; I outlived—sheer miracle—its demons: Kaiser Wilhelm, Franco, Hitler, Stalin, and their heinous ilk, its monstrous wars, gulags, extermination camps, its massacres, genocides, its nuclear sins against the Spirit.

And so it could happen that, in the spring of 1995, the year of the nightmares of Rwanda, East Timor, Tibet, Srebrenica (Bosnia) raging in unabated fury, we sat in Caffe Vivaldi in Greenwich Village talking about that much-touted new millennium just around the corner, that third millennium after Golgotha. What was going to be so "new," starting on January 1, A.D. 2000? Didn't it look more likely to be nothing but a replay of the frightful millennium now limping to its close, perhaps the terminal replay? Is there really nothing to be done, we wondered . . . nothing at all?

Are we doomed; are we condemning ourselves to slide passively into that terminal barbarity? And who were those "we," gathered here around our cappuccinos: humanity's self-appointed representatives, a baker's dozen of U.S. citizens—a few artists, a clergyman, a lawyer, a TV writer and producer, a biologist couple, a nun, a composer, a physicist . . . poor mortals all? Was it all hopeless? Was the real "we," humanity, done for?

"Look," said one of the scientists, "the very fact that we are sitting here, mulling over our predicament, doesn't that mean there is a glimpse of hope? For surely we are not the only ones whose spiritual immune system has not broken down completely. We are not so special! And if we are not so special, there must be millions like us still unaffected by this rabies of the soul, this virus of contempt for life. No, we are not alone!"

"I couldn't agree more," I said, "for I run into them wherever I go, all over this country, Europe, Japan. I meet them where least expected. They are ordinary people as we are, who—against all odds—are still unestranged from their basic human sanity, their capacities for insight, empathy, compassion still intact, and who have not given up on what is human in others. The trouble is that they sit isolated on their little islands, incommunicado, either alone or in little clusters, as we are sitting here, out of contact with the many out there!"

"If that is so," the composer said, "and no doubt it is, we belong to something that could be a powerful antidote to the cynicism and contempt for life, however unorganized, even unorganizable, it may be. So it is actually a matter of establishing real contact, communication among the islands, and that is tough enough, but it is possible!"

"You could call it," said someone else, "an Anti-Barbaric Coalition, A-B C for short, the A-B C of a new beginning."

"Now, let me imagine that we, around this table, are the core of this A-B C, with the formidable task of establishing contact, nay, communication among those millions of islanders. We'd have to realize that such a contact would have to crystallize around something very simple, very basic, to counteract this virus of contempt for life, this obsession with death and with the tools of death that pervades the world."

The words *contempt for life* had fallen again, and that made me think at once of "Reverence for Life," Albert Schweitzer's life motto that he lived from 1915 to his death in 1965. Reverence for Life is the one principle on which a viable ethic can be founded. I saw him apply it in practice while serving on his medical staff in Lambaréné, from 1958 to 1961. Reverence for Life was the guiding principle in everything he did. It was totally free from sentimentality. It was simply the avoidance of inflicting unnecessary suffering on any living being and the alleviation of suffering with all the medical and human means at his disposal. Reverence for the mystery of life was for him the basis not only of an ethic but also of all truly human relationships, not only with our fellow humans, but also with all that lives.

I was drawing the old man, he was eighty-six then, when he sat writing at his desk, his face almost touching the paper, his bristling mustache at times sweeping it as the old hand wrote on, slowly, painstakingly. Once in a while his head would straighten to turn toward the screened window that looked out over the river. Turning back, for an instant aware of me, he mumbled a few words and went on writing. It was getting dark. The file of his pet ants marching across the paper went out of focus in the falling dusk. He stopped his writing, got up stiffly, put on his faded crumpled felt hat, and said, "Let's sit outside."

We sat on the steps of his cabin, mutely watching the dusk deepening on the Ogowe River. He looked worried. "One should have the skin of a hippo," he suddenly grunted without explanation, "and the soul of an angel." His little mongrel Tzu-Tzu sat between us. "Ah! Look at that tree," Schweitzer said after a while, pointing at a kapok in the distance, still gleaming in the setting sun. Then all of a sudden—it sounded at once hopeless and hopeful—"Do you think that the idea of Reverence for Life is really gaining ground?"

I was perplexed. I felt my eyes getting moist. I had just flown across half of a world that seemed to be getting ready to destroy itself in a spasm of violence. What could I say? "Who knows?" I tried. "There is such terrible violence all over, isn't there? Still, you sowed the seed. If anyone did, you did sow the seed."

He sighed . . . "*Ja, ja*" . . . and got up, for the dinner bell was ringing. This happened almost forty years ago, and I am as old now as Schweitzer was then.

What else is it but Reverence for Life that motivated the great prophets of human solidarity in the cruel pandemonium of the twentieth century: Gandhi, Bonhoeffer, Martin Luther King, the Dalai Lama, Bede Griffiths, Archbishop Tutu, Mother Teresa, Laurence VanderPost, Elie Wiesel, Daisetz Teitaro Suzuki, and for me, a non-Catholic, no one more than that genius of the heart Pope John XXIII—among countless lesser known women and men in all parts of the world? What they really have in common, these prophets, must have been a freedom from all cynicism, a love of people, a love of life, and a passionate awe for the mystery called "life," that basically "religious" orientation to existence as such.

"Don't you idealize Schweitzer?" I was asked. "He has been called a paternalist, even a racist."

"I don't idealize him," I said. "He was the product of the colonial era, but literally day and night, for fifty years, he brought medical help where none was available, and he wrote: 'Our task is to do everything possible to protect the human rights of the Africans we have forced to assume the burden of a foreign, technological culture.' He was not just a pioneer of human rights; he was also a pioneer in foreign aid—without any political or ideological strings attached—and a pioneer in missionary work who did not 'convert' anyone, who did not preach Christian love but simply practiced it. At the same time he was a pioneer in practical ecumenism: 'Dogma divides, the Spirit unites,' I heard him stop short a *Time* reporter who started to theologize. And finally, when Schweitzer was in his eighties he was once more the pioneer—the first public figure of his stature to protest vigorously against nuclear testing: 'We are constantly being told about permissible amounts of radiation. Who permits it? Who has the right to permit it?' he wrote. He was a pioneer of the human."

Reverence for Life implies the insight, the empathy and compassion that mark the maturation of the human inner process, and that implies overcoming the split between thinking and feeling that is the bane of our scientism, and the idolization of technology that distances—estranges—us from all emotional and ethical constraints. This same distancing, this objectification of the unobjectifiable, is characteristic of all Realpolitik, racism, ethnic cleansing, cruelty, and exploitation of the other by political, racial, religious collectivized in-group egos, including that free-market mentality for which all that is, is looked upon as mere raw material-for-profit, even if it ruins our species and our earth for generations to come.

Suddenly Caffe Vivaldi seemed invaded by those millions from their isolated little islands, urging us to risk a preliminary attempt at inter-island communication.

No, we are not drifting away from our formidable task of linking the isolated little islands of sanity and humanness. Reverence for Life versus Contempt for Life might well be that basic, simple crystallization point, the link among the innumerable islanders.

"Are you well aware," the scientist asked, "that what we are at the point of embarking on is a very risky experiment? It invites being shrugged off as pitifully naive, ridiculed as paranoid, megalomaniac, or whatever. Moreover, how could we start it if we decide to take the risk, whatever the outcome?"

One thing we agreed upon after lengthy discussion: There was no point at all in starting yet another association or organization complete with PR and fund-raising.

All we could do, we concluded, was simply start by putting ourselves on the line, and so we each committed ourselves to writing directly from the heart—but without excluding the head—on what we consider essential, on That Which Matters, on the criteria of being human or less than human at this technotronic juncture. We would write it as it came, naturally, freely, out of our own life experience, in our own language, professional jargon, or patois, but with a minimum of quotes. And apart from writing this personal credo in a few pages or even a single one, we each undertook to prevail on at least two others we knew to do likewise.

Once we had gathered a few dozen of these intimate, highly personal communications—however varied in viewpoint, tone, and style—we would study them as to their relevance to our shared human condition in this fateful era of transition and would decide whether our harvest merited publication as a living link with our counterparts on their little islands—if only to reassure and encourage them: You are not alone! You are not mad! There are millions of us!

Not only did each of us write that brief paper and inspire others to do the same, but also within a few months we had gathered many more responses than we could have hoped for. The experiment had turned itself into a chain reaction. Most stirring was that whatever the oddities and peculiarities in all these statements, each one commanded full attention and respect. In each one the Vox Humana was clearly audible. Their authors ranged from an archbishop, who, as might be expected, wrote in a somewhat ecclesiastical idiom, to a blues musician who expressed himself in his own idiom, from a Nobel Prize laureate to a woman who founded childcare centers in her own poor black neighborhood, from a composer to a nuclear scientist. Whatever their differences in viewpoint, sophistication, language, style, the common ground of their humanness and of their awareness of their humanness shone through. We did not force those spontaneous contributions into artificial categories. We placed more lyrical writings, poems, tales in the book wherever intuition guided us.

And so the reporting of this chain reaction, far from aspiring to be either entertaining or literary gourmet fare, intends merely to be a timely documentation of resistance to the slide into posthuman barbarism and a sign of hope in the possibility of reestablishing, against all odds, the heart-to-heart contact that bridges our isolation—indeed an act of faith in the survival of our species as a human species.

We pray and trust the chain reaction will not stop with the publication of this book and that it may be no more than its takeoff, for this is no more than the A-B C of a new beginning, born in a coffee shop in Greenwich Village. May it continue to spread across all social, ethnic, geographical borders! For whatever the technological miracles at this change of millennia, the central question facing each of us born on this planet is more than ever: What does it mean to be human?

Rhena Schweitzer Miller

RHENA SCHWEITZER MILLER worked for her father, Albert Schweitzer, at his Lambaréné Hospital in Africa and assumed the hospital's administration after his death. From 1970 to 1999, she assisted her husband, Dr. David Miller, in his work in developing countries.

When you asked me to write, trying to speak out against the horrible barbarism of today, I was at first at a loss for words. What could I possibly have to say that might make a difference? But then, as the daughter of Albert Schweitzer and again reading in your letter: "We know there are still people all over the world who have not given up on humanness of humans, who have not lost contact with the specifically human sanity at their core, and who have maintained a reverence, an awe for the mystery of life," I realized that I could do no better than echo, and perhaps further elucidate a bit, my father's ethical precept of Reverence for Life.

This ethical imperative came to Albert Schweitzer nearly eighty years ago, in his fortieth year, one year after the onset of the First World War, during a trip on the Ogowe River to care for a sick patient. Desperate at the barbarism of the war, he was seeking "a basis in rational thought upon which a viable and ethical civilization could be built." He writes:

> Slowly we crept upstream. Lost in thought I sat on the deck of the barge, struggling to find the elementary and universal conception of the ethical, which I had not discovered in any philosophy. Sheet after sheet I covered with disconnected sentences, merely to keep myself concentrated on the problem. Late on the third day, at the very moment when at sunset we were making our way through a herd of hippopotami, there flashed upon my mind, unforeseen and unsought, the phrase "reverence for life." The iron door had yielded, the path in the thicket had become visible. Now I had found my way to the idea in which affirmation of the world and ethics are contained side by side.

I grew up under his principle of Reverence for Life, which included life in all its forms. I was taught to pick up the drying-out worm on the path and put it back in the grass, not to kill any bugs if not absolutely necessary, not to pick flowers. Later I saw my father's practical realization of Reverence for Life in his hospital-village in the African forest. It was a place where people of all colors, creeds, and nationalities could live together and live in harmony with the domestic and wild animals, where trees and plants were respected, where a life was taken only when it was unavoidable. I, too, lived there for some years, under the spell of the world my father had created. I also had the wonderful experience of spending evenings and nights sitting around a fire with African friends, watching their dances, listening to their songs, feeling very strongly my belonging to the human family, in its diversity and its similarity.

Later I worked with my husband, David, who was a doctor, in many countries of the developing world, and we found ourselves at home in Egypt, Ethiopia, Vietnam, in the Muslim worlds of Yemen and Pakistan, and among the people of Haiti, who in all their misery did not lose their love of life. We worked mostly in villages and found that village people the world over have much in common. They accept you and befriend you when you respect their beliefs and their customs. We have worked in war zones and in famine areas where we were deeply saddened by what we saw. And we found it hard to understand how the same people who could be so friendly could in other circumstances be so cruel.

People unfortunately have killed each other since the beginning of the human race. I don't know how we can surmount the barbarism which seems to get more and more threatening. But certainly being in awe of the wonder of life in all its forms and teaching our children to respect it in all its manifestations, helping them see the beauty of our planet Earth and its inhabitants, can set them on the way toward the creation of a more peaceful and harmonious world.

My credo is expressed in these words of my father: "The deeper we look into nature, the more we recognize that it is full of life, and the more profoundly we know that all life is a secret, and that we are united with all life that is in nature, that all life is valuable, and that we are united with all this life. From this knowledge comes our spiritual relationship to the Universe."

Tenzin Gyatso, the Fourteenth Dalai Lama

I call the high and light aspects
of my being SPIRIT
and the dark and heavy aspects
SOUL.
Soul is at home in the deep,
shaded valleys.
Heavy torpid flowers saturated
with black grow there.
The rivers flow like warm
syrup. They empty into
huge oceans of soul.
Spirit is a land of high, white peaks and glittering jewel-like lakes
and flowers.
Life is sparse and sounds travel great distances.
There is soul music, soul food, and soul love.
People need to climb the mountain not simply because it is
there.
But because the soulful divinity needs to be mated with the
Spirit.

TENZIN GYATSO, the Fourteenth
Dalai Lama, has become a
symbol of a spiritually based
humanism beyond all lines of
religious demarcation. He is a
living sign of hope.

Deep down we must have real affection for each other, a clear recognition of our shared human status. At the same time we must openly accept all ideologies and systems as means of solving humanity's problems. No matter how strong the wind of evil may blow, the flame of truth cannot be extinguished.

Rabbi Avraham Soetendorf

When I was three months old the Gestapo broke into our house in the Jewish "Joden-buurt" quarter in Amsterdam where in 1943 all the Jews had been ordered to live.

The leader of the group watched me, a baby, three months old, and said, "What a pity that this is a Jewish child."

RABBI AVRAHAM SOETENDORF is a national icon in Holland, where his interfaith and ecumenical work are universally respected as expressions of what it means to be truly human.

My father stood up: "How lucky he is, because whatever will happen to him, he will not grow up to be a son of a murderer." The Gestapo hit my father, shouted, and screamed, "Jew-dogs, we will be back to round you up." My father always said that there had been tears in the eyes of the Gestapo leader. These tears saved our lives. That night I was handed over to members of the resistance and my parents went into hiding. A week or so later, a man stood in front of a house in Velp, near Arnhem, with a suitcase. He knocked on the door. A woman, forty-seven years old, German-born, opened the door. He asked her whether she would be prepared to

13

take care of a Jewish baby. If she had said, "It is too dangerous; our neighbors are collaborators with the Nazis; I have an adolescent son; there is a concentration of German soldiers nearby," for all that was true, I, the baby in the suitcase, would not be alive today, would have been one of the one and a half million children that were murdered by the Nazis. But because she opened her door and gave me support and love during the next two terrible war years, I live and work and long for the redemption of the world. My personal story is a universal tale.

God has constituted it in such a way that during the first three or four years of our existence we cannot survive but with the support, protection, and love of others.

Thus it is our human duty as coworkers in God's creation, being created in His image, to assure that all infants will survive and not suffer because of the effects of war, hunger, curable diseases, and pollution. The difference between life and death for millions of children every year is whether the door to massive practical help is opened or closed by humanity. During the last two years I have spoken intimately to tens of thousands of youngsters at schools all over Holland. And I have been exceedingly encouraged.

The surface of egoism, nihilism and the search for money and immediate satisfaction, can easily be broken by one's authentic story. And behind it we find a passion for spiritual values, a willingness to participate actively in endeavors of, for example, Amnesty International, in development projects, ecological efforts, and to combine forces against racism. But this reservoir of hope is not used. On the contrary, the teachers, those who are asked to give positive examples, and among them politicians, are not the teachers of compassion, but the teachers of doom and self-preservation. I feel deep in my heart, in my bones, that we are living in a time that can be called the birth passage of the messianic age.

It is the fiftieth year according to the biblical mode of the Jubilee year, a time when the slaves should be freed, when all debts should be annulled that weigh heavily on so many countries in development, when all wars should be suspended, when all of humankind should share the fruits of the earth. God has given us this sacred time. And time is a gift, if we learn to sanctify it. Whatever was not possible up to now is possible. Whatever efforts for peace were frustrated before will be realized. And it is up to over 4 billion people who have at least an inner link with their various spiritual traditions, 2 billion Christians, over 1 billion Muslims, 1 billion Buddhists and Hindus, Jews, Indians, indigenous people's traditions, etc., to return to their original task of *Tikun Olam*, the restoration of the world. We have to make use of sacred time. We have to see time hold in the profane. I suggest symbolic steps to engender inspiration and willingness to heal the gap between, on the one hand, the politically elected, who complain about lack of public support for courageous acts in order to serve universal goals, like ecological balance, often to contravene national interests, and, on the other hand, the civilians, citizens of the world, who blame the politicians for not showing political will.

With the Dalai Lama, my soul friend, I discussed setting out on a journey of reconciliation. A number of spiritual leaders from the various spiritual traditions would visit places sacred in the various religious cultures like the Wailing Wall and the El Aksa Mosque, the holy graves all in Jerusalem next to one another other, like Mecca, the Vatican, places of the Indians in North America, India, China. In every place representatives of the spiritual tradition that is devoted to this space of holiness would lead a prayer service, and we would all join, to show love that is beyond formal respect.

Yes, there are more roads that lead to the truth. Governments should agree on a budget for the earth, to reassign national budgets in such a way that enough funds would become available to alleviate hunger, provide medical services so that no child will die due to manageable causes. Every citizen would be taxed extra for this universal effort, according to his or her means. Countries and groups within the same national borders that are at odds with each other would suspend all war efforts, in order to join forces in this war on want.

I call upon all spiritual, political, economic, cultural, scientific forces to join in this cooperation with God, the source of all life force. This is the time for reconciliation in the Middle East, in Africa, in Europe, in the whole fractured world. Is it only utopian, a poetic expression of one individual who once has been saved? On the contrary, I believe it is practical and doable.

We have the Universal Declaration of Human Rights, we will soon have an earth charter, delineating our duties toward all living on this planet, and we still hold the various spiritual codes. They all point to our holy task. We don't know why, for God, the crying of a child is more important than all the galaxies, but we know it to be so. The crying should turn into laughter by the end of this millennium, and at least 18 million infants who are sentenced to death, if we stand on the safe pavement and do nothing more than already is done by courageous agencies, should be saved.

And God will bless the work of our hands.

These words are dedicated to Mr. van der Kemp,
who gave his life for my safety on the day of liberation,
5th of May 1945.

Jack Miles

Between religious absolutism and irreligious nihilism stands liberal religion. Naturally, some regard the practice of liberal religion as a milk-and-water concoction compared with the tub-thumping religion of old. And the secular types might find it easier to reject out of hand the old superstitions rather than sit down with a pastor who has a Ph.D. in theology and wants to argue religion. But some want exactly that.

JACK MILES is currently Mellon Visiting Professor of Humanities at the California Institute of Technology. His book *God: A Biography* won a Pulitzer Prize in 1996.

David Tracy, a Catholic theologian at the University of Chicago, has a wonderful phrase describing in a few words the latest stage in our religious evolution: "After enchantment yields to disenchantment," he says, "disenchantment yields to the *disenchantment with disenchantment.*"

In the world that has experienced modernity, some form of liberal religion as an antidote to the disenchantment with disenchantment is where we are headed at the next stage—a religion that doesn't deny the mind while making it possible to recover that sense of awe and ethical obligation that, together, make religion what it is.

I think the day is over when what emerges from one part of the planet can be a religious answer for the whole world.

I would rather expect that all the religious traditions of the world will go into a cultural meat grinder and, after the experience of nihilism has exhausted the spirit, will each manage its own kind of recovery. In our shrinking world, though, these recoveries will influence one another.

The prospects of mutual influence are fascinating to contemplate. Historical religions of protest and prophecy have flowed from Jerusalem, while religions of acceptance and wisdom have flowed from India. Buddhism is the missionary form of Hinduism, Christianity the missionary form of Judaism. The Western way has been not to accept this world and make peace with it, but to change it and make it better. The Eastern view has been to accept the universe as unchangeable, as given. How will all this mesh in one world where we are all rubbing elbows?

In any event, there is no doubt in my mind that a large-scale recovery is under way. Keiji Nishitani wrote this opening line in his book *Religion and Nothingness*: "Man says of religion, 'What good is it?' And religion says to man, 'What good are you?' "

When we ask ourselves the question, as many do today, "What good are we?" we are already in a religious moment. We have already left our confident secularism behind. And, I think, also left behind will be both the naive monotheism and naive polytheism of earlier religious traditions. As I have written in my book *God: A Biography*, the early "drafts" of the Bible offer the image of God that we still find the most powerful. The greatest step any writer makes is the first draft, going from nothing to something. But I also tried to say that God is an evolving character, shaped in dialogue with Himself and His creation.

In this sense, religion is an open-ended enterprise, a continuing dialogue. I have been very influenced by Clifford Geertz, who says that what creates functioning religion is the reflexive relationship it typically establishes between metaphysics and ethics: that is, between the most basic questions of how the world is put together—the question of origins—and how we should conduct ourselves in the world. We act as we do because that is how the world is, and vice versa.

Much social reform proceeds by destroying this kind of relationship, I realize, exposing some presumptively "natural" attitude or behavior as a mere social construct, breaking the very link whose forging forges religion. And much of that destruction is a necessary purification. Still, the assertion that no benign link between fact and value, between nature and conduct, can ever be forged strikes me as gratuitous, an unearned despair or, worse, just a way of ducking the real human assignment. My refusal to despair of such a link is what makes me, secular as I am in so many superficial ways, still a religious man.

Elie Wiesel

ELIE WIESEL is the author of more than thirty internationally acclaimed works of fiction and nonfiction. He is an Andrew W. Mellon Professor of Humanities at Boston University. In 1986 he received the Nobel Peace Prize.

For Jews and Christians alike, as well as for Muslims and all persons of religious faith, being human means—must mean—to see each other's humanity. In other words: I am human not only because I have been given the ability to listen, to speak, to feel pain and joy, but also—and perhaps mainly—because others have been endowed with the same ability. It is the others' humanity that shapes my own.

When, during the darkest of all times, in Nazi-occupied Europe, the enemy treated his victims as subhumans, he deprived himself of his own humanity. No wonder that most laws in Scripture deal with human relations. To believe in God as Creator and Judge of the universe is to accept the concept that all human beings are His subjects and His children. When they are persecuted for any reason, we must see ourselves as their brothers and sisters. To be insensitive to their suffering would drive us away from our common Father.

Thus to be human means to the Jew in me to be concerned with the welfare of my fellow Jews—and then with that of members of other communities.

To the homeless, the poor, the beggar, the victims of AIDS and Alzheimer's, the old and the humble, the prisoners in their prison and the wanderers in their dreams, it is our sacred duty to stretch out our hand and say: "In spite of what separates us, what we have in common is our humanity."

We cannot and must not live isolated from one another. Isolation bequeaths loneliness, whose consequences are not always productive and healthy. That is yet another lesson given to us by Scripture: God alone is alone. Our humanity is measured not by our solitude but by our attitude toward someone else's.

Granted, at times it is not easy to remain human in inhuman circumstances. But then, why should it be?

Yehudi Menuhin

We were granted the greatest
    gifts of all:
        OUR LIFE
        OUR SOUL
        OUR MIND
        AND THE CAPACITY OF
           WONDER.
Nothing was expected in
    return, save to give
        OUR BLESSING
        AND AFFECTION
        AND PROTECTION
as would satisfy a thousand lives.
Yet, we chose to turn our back,
thus betraying TRUST and BEAUTY.
What an ugly transformation into
        CONFRONTATION
        CONDEMNATION
        EXPLOITATION.

YEHUDI MENUHIN
(1916–1999) was not only one
of the world's most admired
musicians but also a humanist and
educator.

We withheld
    OUR BLESSING
    AND AFFECTION
    AND PROTECTION
as would satisfy a thousand lives.
At the threshold of this New Decade
let us turn again, it's not too late,
and start at the beginning:
HONOR ALL LIFE IN ITS VARIETY,
HONOR THE SOUL IN ALL ITS MYSTERY
AND BUILD A NEW WORLD IN OUR MIND,
A HEALTHY WORLD TO LIVE IN FOR MANKIND, and patiently accord
    the passage of all time
its ever-richer harvest of support and inspiration.
Let us give
    OUR BLESSING
    AND AFFECTION
    AND PROTECTION
as would satisfy a thousand lives.

Yehudi Menuhin   23

Mary Evelyn Tucker

MARY EVELYN TUCKER is a professor of religion at Bucknell University, where she teaches courses in world religions, Asian religions, and religion and ecology. She and her husband, John Grim, have directed the series of ten conferences on religions of the world and ecology at the Harvard University Center for the Study of World Religions from 1996 to 1998. They are also editors of the book series from these conferences.

Being human in our times involves the vital sense of renewal with the natural world in its complexity, beauty, and mystery. Our alienation from one another is even more accentuated due to alienation from the earth and from other species. This is no longer a mere romantic or nostalgic call to Thoreau's spirit at Walden Pond but rather a sounding from the depths of the ocean to the heights of the mountains. Our own strangely discordant voices encased in soundproof rooms and reverberating back from television screens have drowned out the subtle sounds of nature.

To be human means to take off the headphones and unplug virtual reality. We need to listen again and to relearn the multiple voices of the universe. From these voices will come the songs of healing and renewal which we will sing with our children and with their children.

If we are to survive as humans, it is crucial that we learn once again to sing.

Oscar Arias

OSCAR ARIAS is a Nobel Prize recipient and former president of Costa Rica.

The ability to show tolerance
in the face of bigotry,
compassion in the face of
indifference,
moral fortitude in the face of
complex decisions,
is one way of expressing our humanness.
As we approach the dawn of a new millennium,
we must remember that our ability to reason, reflect,
and undertake conscientious decisions
will mark the posterity of our race.
Thus the art of being humane will be
the artistry of maintaining our future.

Facundo Cabral

Our grandparents told us the story of how long ago the leader of our town government, who was far from being a tyrant, had been elected because he was the best human being available. So the people put both the present and the future of our town in his hands, but in the long run he got more and more tired of everyone agreeing with

FACUNDO CABRAL is an internationally known Argentine singer, composer, and troubadour for the human condition. He has several platinum and gold records and has performed in more than forty countries throughout the world.

him all the time, being waited on hand and foot by the loveliest beauty queens, and no one allowing him to lose at poker games. He was desperate to resign, but that was out of the question, and so the solitude of power was bound to kill him. Before he died, his exceptionally noble soul enacted the most loving, most beautiful laws ever heard of, for he had loved all that was good and beautiful in life. These are the decrees he left behind:

I ORDER that in this town nothing should ever be held to be more valuable than life itself, so that we can go hand in hand seeking for Truth.

I ORDER that every weekday be as bright and luminous as any Sunday.

I DECREE that every house be outfitted with flower boxes and that their windows should be kept open to catch the green songs of spring.

I DECREE that everyone free him- or herself from all lies and take off all masks of secrecy so that all can sit down together and talk of beauty and of justice.

I DECREE that more attention be paid to Isaiah the prophet's "The lamb and the lion will lie together" and that the food they share will have the fragrance of the dawn.

I ORDER that all bread be flavored with tenderness, that joy will be our town's banner and love its only armament.

AND STARTING TODAY ALL MONEY WILL CARRY AN EXPIRATION DATE SO THAT NO ONE CAN ACCUMULATE IT TO BUY POWER AND DOMINION OVER OTHERS.

THERE WILL BE ONLY ONE ARISTOCRACY, THAT OF THE SPIRIT, AND ONLY ONE PRIVILEGE, THAT OF INTELLIGENT IMAGINATION.

Dorothea Sölle

"Reverence for Life" in the sub-
title of this volume immediately speaks to my heart,
because most of my work—as a
theological writer in Germany
after the Shoah—is about
learning the A-B-C of human culture in different perspectives. In
my understanding, the third millennium began in 1989 with the
final victory of the free market and the globalization of markets and
media. Since then I try to get "alphabetized" in economics, because
I don't understand why it is that the rich get richer on every day
God makes and the poor, and more of them, get more miserable. I
read in the Good Book: "He who oppresses a poor person, insults
his or her Maker" (Proverbs 14:31).

Economic and ecological alphabetization is on the agenda for all
of us. We are to learn how to read the message of the victims of our
ways of living, eating, heating, traveling, working, consuming, and
even dying. The victims of our *Lebenswelt*, among them Mother
Earth, constitute this hidden, sometimes obvious barbaric reality
which we have created and do enjoy. "Reading" means not only

DOROTHEA SÖLLE is a highly
respected German feminist,
theologian, and author.

29

listing the evils our media daily feed us with. It also means to ask those simple questions like: Who needs the new machine that kills again some hundreds of jobs? Who sets the agenda for what is called interest-free scientific research? Who benefits from the current "new world order"?

In my home state in Germany, the Rhineland, right now ten thousand teachers are lacking. There are enough unemployed teachers around. But why should anyone invest in education? The government still believes in Eurofighters. I think Bertolt Brecht was right in stating, "Evil has an address. It has a telephone number." To learn to read means to know addresses and numbers.

This process of learning to read the A-B-C works only when we learn at the same time to write it down. I am not referring here to my personal job as word producer but to our whole being as creative visible members of the world community. How will we learn to "write," to make ourselves visible, audible, touchable?

In my view, our "writing" on the walls of our prisons and in the book of life as well has two different addresses. I hesitate to name one of them first and the other second, because our learning to "write" is one act. One address of our writing is the public audience. To mention just an example: Remember the mothers of the disappeared in Buenos Aires. In walking in silence on the Plaza de Mayo every Thursday they "wrote" the message into the hearts of the bystanders. Being a German, I know what this word *bystander* means. The letters we should learn to write with our lives rarely reach out to those in power. They may be understood by those bystanders inviting them to become agents of their own lives again.

The other address to write to does not show in the phone book. But I think we all know a manner of wishful thinking which the tradition called prayer. To learn to "write" is a way to clarify our deepest wishes and hopes. Writing those letters to the Nameless One will not change the barbaric culture in which we live. But it may change us, keeping our dreams alive, sharing our visions. And in prayer we may share our healing stories, such as "Robben Island today is not a concentration camp any longer." We begin to give thanks.

A-B-C to me means that we learn to read and write. I wish my whole life were filled with this reading of reality from the perspective of the losers and the writing down of those dreams of a different life. The themes for which we need alphabetization are named in my tradition of the Ecumenical movement with three beautiful names:

- justice—or a different economic world order
- peace—built upon more justice, not on violence
- integrity of creation

Together they are called a conciliar process, because right now we are still in this barbaric war against the poor, ourselves, and our mother. Learning to spell A-B-C-D-E-F-G will happen in singing a different tune.

Thomas Berry

THOMAS BERRY is a historian of cultures, with special concern for the foundation of human cultural traditions in the natural world. He is author of *The Dream of the Earth*.

Like most other persons in these last years of the twentieth century, I have given some thought to where we are, what is happening, and what our human prospects for the coming century are. My first thoughts have been that human affairs have changed mightily since the ending of World War II in 1945. While this change is seen most dramatically in space travel, computer skills, medical technologies, genetic manipulation, astronomical discoveries, and the plastics industries, it is also obvious in food production, transportation, altered economic values, the rise of over a hundred new nations in the political order, the new religious orientations. So, too, there is the change in moral values, in relations of humans with one another, in gender roles, in family structure, in education, in the media, entertainment, and the arts.

In all of this there is somehow a feeling that we humans are now in control of the world about us. We are outsmarting the planet in its own proper functioning. Outsmarting the atomic and nuclear structures by invading their inmost reality. Outsmarting gravitation by our ventures into space. Outsmarting the forests as regards the real purpose of their existence. Outsmarting the land by teaching it how to grow immense quantities of nourishing food for humans. Outsmarting the marine life of the oceans that seek to evade our capture. Outsmarting the chemical balance of the planet by producing 200 million tons of industrial chemicals each year that nature knows nothing about.

We are so captivated with this power of control over the planet that we mercilessly continue our assault on the planet even when the Earth is obviously becoming wasted, worn, deformed, and progressively dysfunctional, its beauty disfigured. Yet there is an obstinate refusal to withdraw from our technological triumphalism in favor of a little sober reflection, even perhaps a moment of foreboding. These outsmarting processes are all done by our scientific and engineering technologies for the purpose of fostering human well-being but also for economic gain in favor of the corporate enterprise and its organizing personnel. The quest for human well-being is itself subverted for economic gain on a somewhat monstrous scale.

The ultimate issue before the human community is no longer the challenge of religious dominance, as was the possibility in the earlier phases of European history. Nor is it the imperial dominance of the predemocratic period. Nor is it now the threat of the dominance sought by National Socialism. Nor is it the Fascist dominance that derives ultimately from Roman authoritarian tradition. Nor the dominance of Leninist Communism. The controlling force of the present might be identified as Economism. We are dealing with the quest for dominance over both the human and the natural worlds by corporate economic powers, with the subservience of democratic political structures.

The meetings at Bretton Woods during World War II that set up the economic patterns for the postwar planet provided the basis for the easy acceptance of the World Bank and the International Monetary Fund. These enabled the corporation to substitute economic colonialism carried out by the new industrial empires in place of the political colonialism of prewar nation-states. This new economic colonialism has been further confirmed by the more recent GATT treaties and the World Trade Organization. The political order on both the national and international scale now subserves economic processes.

These corporations now own the planet. They own the governments: the legislatures, the executives, and judiciaries. In some sense they own the people. They provide the jobs that produce the goods that the people buy with the wages they earn in the production process while the benefits accrue to the owners and managers. This corporate enterprise directly or indirectly determines the professions of law and medicine and education and whatever. Whether it is wealth or human well-being that is the determining motive in this effort at human takeover of the planetary direction, the consequence is the same.

The ultimate quest of the corporate enterprise is to take over the integral functioning of the planet itself—in some sense to take over the functioning of the universe, for the solar system in which the earth functions is itself controlled by the more comprehensive order of the universe. Thus our contemporary human community is ultimately concerned not simply with political control of the human community or with economic control over the earth but with control over the deeper physics of the universe itself.

While this is not an explicit aim, it is the deeper implication of what is happening at the present time throughout the entire range of human presence on the planet. Our contemporary difficulty, which must be dealt with at the close of this millennium, is this radical sense that the human and the natural worlds are more adversarial than cooperative and that the human, to avoid being controlled and oppressed by the natural world, must learn not only to control but to reshape the functioning of the planet Earth in a more benign relationship with humans. This amounts not simply to a reeducation of the earth and even of the universe, but also a remaking of the total range of existence.

This we seek to accomplish by the alliance of sciences and technologies under the direction of corporations that have already gotten control over the human community. Beyond the human the control over the planet has been established.

Our effort to outsmart the earth in its various modes of functioning leads ultimately to our effort to outsmart the universe.

This is the issue before us at the end of one millennium and the beginning of another. Will we humans accept the universe as the controlling context of existence, or will we insist that the human be accepted as the controlling context of existence? Controlling implies the setting of limits and determining patterns of relationship. Will we accept our status as functioning within the greater community of existence or will we humans insist that the greater community of existence accept its status within the determinations imposed by the human?

Nothing can be more important than the integral functioning of the universe, for everything in the universe is dependent on the proper functioning of the universe in its large-scale structure, just as all life in the solar system is dependent on the sun for its light and warmth. If gravitation were to disappear, then the universe would immediately disintegrate. If gravitational attraction overcame the differentiating impetus of the universe, then the universe would collapse. In this sense nothing is more important than the preservation of these fundamental principles on which the universe depends for both its existence and its functioning.

It takes little thought and only a moment's observation to appreciate the success of the universe and of the planet Earth in the immense variety and vitality of their productions in their prehuman phase. The vigor and diversity of life expressions throughout the earth are especially convincing to even a limited view. Now at the end of this century when we look at the planet we can only wonder at the devastation that we have inflicted, the ruined rivers, the ruined soils, the ruined oceans, the ruined atmosphere—all witness to the failed efforts to improve the functioning of the planet in its service of the humans. Now we witness the dying of the great forests of the earth as recently documented by Charles Little in his book *The Dying of the Trees*. We witness the chemical poisoning of the planet and the distortions brought about in the genetic functioning of the humans in the book entitled *Our Stolen Future*.

Comparing the earth, and its magnificence prior to this century, to the earth as it presently exists, after all the outsmarting of the planet attempted by humans, can only lead to the conclusion that what we think we are doing and what we are really doing are quite different things. Outsmarting earth is a more risky thing than we bargained for. We do not really have the knowledge or the skills needed to control the functioning of the planet.

The conclusion should be that the universe and the planet Earth are consistently more effective than humans can ever be. The beginning of wisdom is to accept us as component members of the larger earth community and of the universe itself, then to accept our instructions from the natural world about us and to fulfill our role within this context.

In carrying out this program of actions there are three basic conditions that need to be established. The first condition is recognition that the universe is composed of subjects to be communed with, not objects to be exploited. Every mode of being has its own inner spontaneity, its capacity to evoke wonder and praise from every other being. This inner spontaneity provides that "person" aspect of the various modes of being. It is what establishes the inherent rights that every living being especially possesses. For every being has the right to be, the right to habitat, and the right to fulfill its role in the great community of existence. These rights are distinctive to the various modes of being. Trees have tree rights, rivers have river rights—the right not to be thwarted in its need to flow freely, the right to be free from pollution that kills its life forms. So with every other mode of being.

The second condition is recognition that the human is a subsystem of earth, which is the base system. The earth community has an absolute priority in our concern over any other member, or group of members of the planet. The well-being of any member of the planetary community is derivative from the well-being of the planet. If the planet is damaged, every being on the planet suffers. In virtue of this condition the primary law of economics must be the preservation of the integrity of the earth economy. To think that we can have a rising gross domestic product with a declining gross earth produce is obviously absurd. So with medicine and so with any other human function. We cannot have well humans on a sick planet. If the planet is dysfunctional, then this will affect every being on the planet.

The third condition is recognition that the planet earth will never again function the way it has functioned in the past. In the past the planet brought forth the superabundance of life expression totally independent of humans since humans did not exist. In the future, however, almost nothing will happen on the planet that humans will not be involved in. While we cannot make a blade of grass, there is liable not to be a blade of grass if humans do not accept it, protect it, foster it, and assist in healing the damaged conditions of its survival.

Such are the conditions. We need remember one other fact. The planet earth is a onetime event. Earth has its basic endowment, its quantum of creative energies. With the light and warmth and energy of the sun it must shape its future, heal what is damaged, and continue its pattern of creative life expression. Just what the possibilities are we do not know. We only know that the past will not repeat itself. It will never come again. Extinct species will never return.

There is one lesson we should learn from our experience of the twentieth century: Our efforts to outsmart earth will only bring about disastrous consequences.

(Translated by Frederick Franck and Janis Roze)

José Muñoz

Remember that capacity of imagining fantasy worlds where we rode imaginary steeds, rescued lost causes as in quixotic dreams, drummed a sonata on the dining room table imagining we were giving a brilliant concert? Such things are part of

JOSÉ MUÑOZ is president of CORPRODIC, a Colombian educational and research organization working with the Indians of Colombia.

our intimate treasury, impenetrable for others yet pointing in the direction of life's meaning.

Soon, all too soon, this world of the imagination collides with the adult world of priests, soldiers, policemen, wheeler-dealers, censors, parents. We are conditioned, programmed, brainwashed to the point where barbarism starts with approved vernacular, with acceptable hypocrisies and the conventional lies that have become habitual as correct ways of thinking, of repressing laughter, where laughter would be our only defense. It is around this time that the preachers of "truth" loom up, the ones who possess and dispense their dogmas, impose their superiority posture as unique models to be imitated. The media belong here, those defenders of society, who keep it all together by propagating consumption, by creating needs, by hypnotizing the consumer to buy—by all the means at their disposal, political and psychological—by exploiting national and ethnic identities, propagating hostility toward "the other," all who differ from us by being Indian or peasant or black or Southerners or Northerners, by being either First or Third World aliens.

What is left of the children we once were? Fragments, memories, scents from the time our sensitivity was still intact, before it was coarsened by contact and adaptation to the adult, the programmed adult, incarnation of brutality. In Colombia young people have for the past half-century had few other options than to pick up arms, any kind of arms, as if prescribed by some sacrosanct dogma or perhaps without any other dogma than the fact that the easiest way to make money is to terrorize others, a way of making one's living. But this violence has already been programmed by their earliest conditioning and by the fear instilled in them of ever becoming what they dreamed of becoming. At the same time they are taught to despise, to consider as inferior and expendable, those "others," women not excluded, of course.

When I was working with and learning from our Colombian Indians, I kept wondering why they were so different from us. They did not seem to worry about the meaning of life; they just lived it to the full. I saw their reverence for all existence. It was visible in the way they handled things, without arrogance, without sentimentality. To recover such sensitivity is to recover reverence for life, and this may well be our most urgent task—to reawaken a sense of beauty, the beauty of the land at dawn, of flowers unfolding, of the fragrances of festive Christmas meals and family reunions.

This love of life, this reverence, has been expressed in innumerable poems and myths, in the epics of six thousand cultures that still survive on earth, in the traditional wisdom that is not yet totally forgotten. The real task of education is to reawaken these sensitivities, to stimulate their unfolding by creating an environment that nurtures them. Then one day there may be an explosion of artistic and scientific creativity, of constructive discrimination between what demeans and what gives dignity to life and confirms our harmony with the universe. I do believe that we can free ourselves from being slaves to today's barbarity and recapture the essence of being humanly alive.

C. Richard Chapman

C. RICHARD CHAPMAN is professor in the departments of anesthesiology, psychiatry, and behavioral sciences at the University of Washington. His special area of expertise is research on pain and suffering.

Who are we? What are we? have intrigued us humans long before the beginnings of recorded history. Late in 1994, I was fascinated reading about an archaeological treasure just found in southern France at Vallon Pont d'Arc. It consists of a vast network of caves the walls of which are covered with paintings and engravings of the Paleolithic Age, some twenty thousand years ago. Looking at photographs of these images of animals and symbols one can't help wondering what motivated these ancient hunter-artists. Were they already asking themselves "Who are we?," trying to define their identity in confrontation with these mammoths, ibexes, panthers, and bears they drew, coming to terms with their struggle for survival, matching their crude weapons against the tooth and claw of their fellow predators?

It is disturbing to look back into this carnivorous world and realize that as far as we know, the brain of these hunters of twenty thousand years ago was biologically identical with our contemporary human brain. And since the brain may be considered our "behavioral organ," it might explain the survival of behavior patterns similar to that of the mammoth hunters of Pont d'Arc. On the other hand, this similarity justifies assuming that not only the artistic potentialities were already present in these cavemen but also those potentialities, from philosophy and theology to oil paintings and oratorios, which grace our culture but do not quite compensate for our biological imperative for barbarity, aggression, and senseless killing, still all too dominant, judged by the six o'clock news, day after day. When the ice retreated and the great beasts withdrew, humans took to killing one another for territory and social power. Proud of their biological imperative for mayhem, Bronze Age artists celebrated conquests and victories in their bas-reliefs. In later centuries they depicted triumphantly the execution and/or the enslavement of the losers. Since the Renaissance, artists have become famous glorifying the savagery of battle in oils, until, in our time, our chief amusement seems to consist in movies and videotapes of a continuum of those confrontations as the most profitable asset of the entertainment industry.

On the threshold of the twenty-first century our "struggle with nature" is about over. Our scientific and technical triumphs are awesome. We have walked on a moon which endless generations of ancestors could only stare at in impotent wonder. We send probes to the farthest reaches of the solar system. Our quantum mechanics and particle physics are penetrating the secrets of matter. Medical science and technologies rescue our sick from ever more crippling diseases. Intoxicated with success, we have become future-obsessed and dream of even greater accomplishments.

Long, long ago we developed a kind of conscience. Systems of human values were expressed in codes of ethics. And yet we still kill one another with bizarre supersonic brutality. During this century we have massacred one another on an unprecedented global scale on the pretext of ill-defined superstitions, short-term political gains, and even the honor of God. If the signals we are sending into space hoping to contact extraterrestrial intelligent life hit their targets and such intelligent life has in turn detected and observed us, we don't have to fear invasion—even if minimally intelligent, they would prudently avoid all contact with our dangerous planet.

And yet, if we were indeed totally barbaric, inherently malicious, would we have the urge to reflect upon ourselves with a sense of moral indignation? There must therefore be another side to our nature, capable, at times, of true compassion for one another and even for other living things. Don't we collectively cling to the belief that brutality is not all there is to us, even a persistent faith that every human being has a foundational potentiality for levels of consciousness not exclusively linked to individual and collective survival?

Most of us experience this level of awareness only in brief glimpses. It eludes scientific description and analysis but is as spontaneous and nonrational as it is ineradicable and meaningful. To call it spiritual might be to pigeonhole it as "religiosity," but this intuitive awareness might be even more basic, even more profound. It might point at the very core of our specifically human nature, deeply embedded in the fathomless depths of our consciousness. Anyone aware of this intuition is simply unable to denigrate, exploit, let alone murder, a fellow human being.

Nancy Willard

Out of War

In the forest a soldier sees a
    child asleep and a fox
rocking the cradle.
The great paws sheathe

blades curved like sickles,
    gentle as moths
for rocking. The man waits,
his hand on the new grenades

that he came to throw
in the forest where
no one lives
save a child and a slow

NANCY WILLARD is an award-winning author whose books include *Swimming Lessons: New and Selected Poems*; a novel, *Sister Water*; and a collection of essays, *Telling Time: Angels, Ancestors and Stories*. She teaches at Vassar College.

fox with its great claws
curled for catching
small fish and berries
and leaves. They pause,

the fox and his clever
enemy, the man who wants
someone to kill; surely
that would restore whatever

it is he's lost, the weather
of inward mornings, of play,
between fox and man's child, of how
they lie down together.

Joseph Rotblat

I am a man of peace. This, of course, is to be expected from a Nobel Peace Prize laureate. I am also a pacifist. I abhor war. I dislike any resort to violence, but I am not an absolute pacifist. I do not exclude the possibility that in some circumstances I might find myself involved in activities that violate my prin-

JOSEPH ROTBLAT is emeritus professor of physics at the University of London. He is a Fellow of the Royal Society and former president of Pugwash. In 1995 he received the Nobel Peace Prize.

ciples. I would describe myself as a realistic pacifist.

But, some of you might say, this is an oxymoron.

I am not an absolute pacifist, because I do not believe in absolutes. Nature is so rich in its variety, there being an infinite number of possibilities, that nothing can be excluded.

By the same token, anything that we aim at should be possible. Even if at first it seems out of this world, it can materialize, if sufficient faith and effort is put into it.

An example is the concept of a world without war. This is the central theme of my work. My abhorrence of war stems from personal experience of the two world wars of this century. In the first, as a young child I suffered extreme privation: hunger, cold, filth, contagious diseases, in the full meaning of these words. Such experience in one's formative years is never forgotten.

In the Second World War there was the danger of being hit by a German bomb in the nightly air raids on Liverpool. But worse than this was the moral anguish about abandoning moral values. I'll talk more about this later.

But to these two reasons for my call to abolish war—the physical suffering and breakdown of moral standards—I want to add another, overwhelming reason: the threat to human life on this planet.

Whatever view you may hold about the origins of human life—whether we take literally the biblical version that it was the deed of God on the sixth day of creation or hold the rationalist notion that it was the outcome of an infinite number of seemingly random changes in the configuration of chemical compounds over billions of years, either originating on this earth or arriving from other places in the universe on the tail of a comet—we all agree that life is our most precious commodity.

We don't dare to think that it might be brought to an end, least of all by the action of man. Yet the unimaginable is now possible. The survival of the human species can no longer be taken for granted. The human species is now an endangered species.

Actually, the extinction of the human species has always been a possible, but extremely unlikely, event. It was thought of as a result of some cataclysmic occurrence, such as the collision with an asteroid or a comet or an exceptionally violent volcanic eruption. It is believed that the extinction of some animal species that once dominated the planet, such as the dinosaurs, was due to some such event, although views still differ about its precise nature. But the fact that this catastrophe occurred 65 million years ago and none of such magnitude has been recorded since means that, for all practical purposes, we can put it out of our minds.

That the extinction of the human race would be created by the action of man was never considered seriously.

History is full of instances of terrible slaughter in war. We are supposed to become more civilized, yet the largest carnage in absolute terms has taken place in this century. Eight and a half million dead was the direct result of the First World War. In the Second World War some 55 million died. More than 20 million lives were lost in the many wars since then, mostly in the developing countries. Above all, the greatest ever single crime of genocide was committed during the Second World War, when the Nazis carried out a scientifically designed program of systematic elimination of a whole category of people for no reason other than that they were members of certain races.

However, even such heinous designs never succeeded in full, for various reasons, mainly technical. But the technical obstacles have been removed by the onset of the omnicidal weapons first demonstrated in 1945 in Hiroshima and Nagasaki. The destruction of these cities opened a new age, the nuclear age.

One of the chief characteristics of the nuclear age is that for the first time in the history of civilization it became possible for man to destroy his own species. And to accomplish it, willfully or inadvertently, in a single action. It's very difficult for any rational person to imagine such a monstrous deed being allowed to happen.

The only way to remove permanently the risk of ultimate catastrophe is to abolish war altogether. War must cease to be an admissible social institution. We must learn to resolve our disputes by means other than military confrontation.

Many will say that the elimination of war is complete fantasy, a utopian dream that will never be fulfilled. There are even schools of thought that maintain that aggressiveness is genetically built into human nature. I do not accept this. I do not believe that there is scientific evidence that biology condemns humanity to war.

However, for the concept of a war-free world to become a reality a process of education would be required aimed at making people think about security in global terms. Our traditional upbringing has taught us to think of security in terms of our nation. We accept the need for a strong military force to protect our nation from attack by other nations. In the new situation, where a conflict anywhere may escalate and endanger all humanity, it is in everybody's interest, including our national interest, to prevent any conflict in any part of the world from developing into a military confrontation. No nation can be allowed to start a war, because any war can become a threat to the whole of humanity. Protection of the human race must take precedence over other interests. Even if it incurs giving up some national sovereignty.

The fantastic advances in communication and transportation have shrunk our globe. We are creating a truly interdependent global community. We have acquired the means to establish close cultural bonds. We can get to know each other better, thanks to many electronic networks.

We have the technical means, the technical tools, to foster a feeling of belonging to humankind, to pave the way toward the main goal, a world of peace.

But ultimately the decisions about global security will be made by the politicians, and it is particularly the leaders of the nuclear states that would seem to be in need of education in these matters.

Throughout the centuries we have tried to ensure that we have peace by preparing for war. And throughout the centuries we had war. Even in the nuclear age, when any war carries the threat of ultimate catastrophe, the nuclear path follows the same concept, by accumulating enormous nuclear arsenals. It is of the utmost importance to recognize the folly of this policy and adopt a new policy: *Si vis pacem, para pacem.* (If you want peace, prepare for peace.) This is the way to safeguard our most precious property, humankind. This must be our motto.

The creation of a war-free world will take a very long time to achieve. But we will never achieve it unless we make a start. I appeal to you and to all citizens of the world, remember your humanity.

Charlie Musselwhite

Real emotion moves me. When I hear real feelings expressed in music I sense the human connection.

My earliest recollection of blues is hearing it in Memphis as a kid in the fifties. It came from the black workers in the fields along Cyprus Creek near the dead-end road I lived on with my mother. The emotion I felt in that music wrapped itself around me and touched my heart. It was very comforting. It gave my loneliness and sadness a sweetness. A kind of hope.

CHARLIE MUSSELWHITE is a Mississippi-born blues artist whose music crosses the lines of blues, jazz, and rock. His recording career began in the 1960s in Chicago and has continued for more than thirty years with performances throughout the world.

Their blues expressed how I felt, too. My parents were divorced; I was an only child; I felt alone as my mother worked long and late hours. I was adrift and out of place when blues floated in like a dream and touched my heart. The blues rescued me.

That's when the blues overtook me. Over the years blues have continued to express how I feel as a human being. Now, more than forty years later, as I work as a blues musician, the music I heard as a kid is still with me; it is a kind of antidote to all the things around us that lack compassion. Blues is a music of the heart. It expresses all human emotions; everything life can throw at you—all the ups and downs—it's all in there.

When you hear the blues it reminds your heart what it means to be human.

Václav Havel

It seems to me that one of the most basic human experiences, one that is genuinely universal and unites—or, more precisely, could unite—all of humanity, is the experience of transcendence in the broadest sense of the word.

Today we are in a place and facing a situation to which classically modern solutions do not give a satisfactory response. After all, the very principle of inalienable human rights, conferred on man by the Creator, grew out of the typically modern notion that man—as a being capable of knowing nature and the world—was the pinnacle of creation and lord of the world.

This modern anthropocentrism inevitably meant that He who allegedly endowed man with his inalienable rights began to disappear from the world. He was so far beyond the grasp of modern science that He was gradually pushed into the sphere of privacy of

VÁCLAV HAVEL is a playwright and author whose role in the struggle for human rights and freedoms in Eastern Europe led him to become president of the Czech Republic and a voice for humanity throughout the world.

sorts, if not directly into a sphere of private fancy—that is, to a place where public obligations no longer apply. The existence of a higher authority than man himself simply began to get in the way of human aspirations.

The idea of human rights and freedoms must be an integral part of any meaningful world order. Yet I think it must be anchored in a different place and in a different way than has been the case so far.

In a science that is new—postmodern—ideas are being produced that in a certain sense allow science to transcend its own limits. I will give two examples. The "anthropic cosmological principle" brings us to an idea, perhaps as old as humanity itself, that we are not at all just an accidental anomaly, the microscopic caprice of a tiny particle whirling in the endless depths of the universe. Instead, we are mysteriously connected to the universe, we are mirrored in it, just as the entire evolution of the universe is mirrored in us.

The moment it begins to appear that we are deeply connected to the entire universe, science reaches the outer limits of its powers. With the anthropic cosmological principle, science has found itself on the border between science and myth. In that, however, science has returned, in a roundabout way, to man and offers him his lost integrity. It does so by anchoring him once more in the cosmos.

The second example is the "Gaia hypothesis." This theory brings together proof that the dense network of mutual interactions between the organic and inorganic portions of the earth's surface form a single system, a kind of megaorganism, a living planet, Gaia, named after an ancient goddess recognizable as an archetype of the Earth Mother in perhaps all religions.

According to the Gaia hypothesis, we are parts of a greater whole. Our destiny is not dependent merely on what we do for ourselves but also on what we do for Gaia as a whole. If we endanger her, she will dispense with us in the interests of a higher value—life itself. What makes the anthropic principle and the Gaia hypothesis so inspiring? One simple thing: Both remind us of what we have long suspected, of what we have long projected into our forgotten myths and what perhaps has always lain dormant within us as archetypes. That is, the awareness of our being anchored in the earth and the universe, the awareness that we are not here alone or for ourselves alone but are an integral part of higher, mysterious entities against whom it is not advisable to blaspheme.

This forgotten awareness is encoded in all religions. All cultures anticipate it in various forms. It is one of the things that form the basis of man's understanding of himself, of his place in the world, and ultimately of the world as such.

The only real hope of people today is probably a renewal of our certainty that we are rooted in the earth and, at the same time, the cosmos. This awareness endows us with the capacity for self-transcendence.

Politicians at international forums may reiterate a thousand times that the basis of the new world order must be universal respect for human rights, but it will mean nothing as long as the imperative does not derive from the respect of the miracle of being, the miracle of the universe, the miracle of nature, the miracle of our own existence.

It follows that, in today's multicultural world, the truly reliable path to peaceful coexistence and creative operation must start from what is the root of all cultures and what is infinitely deeper in human hearts and minds than political opinions, antipathies, or sympathies and must be rooted in self-transcendence.

Richard Connolly

RICHARD CONNOLLY, a writer and producer, is director of the communication media arts program at SUNY Rockland Community College.

To be human is to be in transformation. Ever-changing, we are connected by physical, mental, emotional, and spiritual forces more powerful than ourselves.

We experience each moment of our lives with a sense of our relative powerlessness. We choose what we do within the limits of time and space, culture and society, this and that.

As we live our lives, moment to moment, awareness of our powerlessness can, paradoxically, empower us and can allow us to see what and who and where we really are. This awareness is possible in each moment.

With this specifically human awareness, our capacity for empathy and compassion connects us, consciously and unconsciously, to other human beings, to other living things, to all of life.

HERE WE ARE . . . .

Daniel Martin

An eagle rejoices in the oak
    trees of heaven
Crying
This is what I wanted
       —James Wright

I believe that everything is part
and expression of the unfolding
of a mysterious, formless source
that we refer to by many
names, though in the end it is
always the Nameless One.

DANIEL MARTIN is an independent consultant in the area of personal and organizational change and development. A native of Belfast, he worked for ten years as a priest in Kenya. Since 1984 he has been director of the Institute on Global Issues.

There is no one thing that completely manifests this formless source; rather, all things together give expression to the One.

However, the stars show the power of the One, while the earth expresses its marvelous diversity. Flowers manifest the beauty of the One, while animals reveal its gracefulness. In humans, the One expresses itself in self-reflective awareness and consciousness.

The miracle of life's unfolding is through a process of complexification, whereby simple form gives way first to chaos and then to newer, richer, more complex form. This is also the process of the development of self-reflective consciousness in us humans. The ultimate realization of all forms is a return to the formless source through a series of deaths and rebirths, whereby the old stages die as a prelude to resurrection in the next stage. Beyond the final realization, there is the possibility of yet further expressions of the formless One.

We humans play a distinct role in this process as the most recent expression of the formless One. In us, all forms find their realization, in the sense that everything moves toward the more complex level of life that we are calling consciousness. In a sense, we humans live on behalf of all other forms of life; in our own consciousness the whole universe of forms can find expression. From this realization have come the various notions about the role and dignity of the human.

We humans, as the most recent expression of the great unfolding of life, are relative newcomers on the cosmic scene. The birth of self-reflective consciousness has happened over a long period. The process is analogous to the maturation of an individual who grows through the stages of sense perception, image construction, verbal development, individual separation, and, hopefully, complete reintegration of all previous stages into a universal sense of self. With each stage, this process has accelerated its speed of development.

The future, it would appear, from glimpses that the more mature of the species have been blessed with, will consist of further stages of consciousness, including conscious connection with all other life-forms, identification with the essential qualities of life (the archetypes), and cosmic or universal self-realization.

For the present, however, we humans seem to be stuck in the stage of individual or ego identity which, because of its seductive as well as familiar nature, causes us to cling to this stage and to fear and reject the necessary completion or death that allows the next stage to be realized. I see this fearful immobility as the root of all our present problems, both environmental and social, for we have built what has become the dominant culture of the planet on the illusion of separation from and superiority over the rest of life.

The solution to our problems, therefore, is the realization of the process of life's unfolding in and through us. Our role, then, is to foster the unfolding of the next level of consciousness and the emergence of the new era it will bring with it. This will be an era of conscious interconnectedness, not only between humans but also between humans and other life-forms.

We can participate in this unfolding through appreciating the new framework or cosmology. It is this story-become-myth, through the contributions of various, related movements—feminist, indigenous, mystical—that will be the foundation for the next stage of human unfolding. It is this story that will also provide the context within which to appreciate the intuitions (revelations) of the past and allow them, in turn, to inspire our lives again today.

To foster the new stage of life's unfolding, we will articulate the principles that this new story reveals, These principles will be founded on the dynamics or observed patterns of the universe unfolding itself: diversity, interiority/subjectivity, and communion. They will include things like beauty, the value of all forms of life, interconnectedness, the responsibilities and the rights of all humans. From these principles will be distilled renewed values like humility, simplicity, sustainability, community, and trust. These values, in turn, will produce the kind of ethics that will guide human behavior and shape human lifestyles, institutions, and struc-tures for a new and sustainable future. I see my own life, its work, its play, its relationships, within this context. I feel passionately about my own particular role as teacher and guide for the next stage of human and cosmic unfolding. This work is especially significant now amidst the last spasms of the old individual-self stage, even though the new forms, roles, and structures have not yet emerged.

I believe I need to live and become this growing realization more deeply in everything I do, and then I have to join with others everywhere to create new forms, systems, and structures that will appropriately express and support it.

I need, therefore, to foster a new sensitivity in myself, by learning to be maximally present to the basic aspects of existence, to the ordinary things of everyday life, like eating, relating, and recreating. Through such firsthand—primary—experience I will be shaped by the power of life itself. I also believe that the insights and intuitions of all the great faiths, as well as the traditions of the arts, remind me on a deep level—stir the deep, common memory— of who I am and thereby open me to the movement of life's unfolding and to constructive action.

The emerging principles of life that I mentioned I would describe as meta-religious, in the sense that they embrace all the perspectives of faith but also call these to new levels of meaning in the face of today's challenges. They are the essential ecological foundation of truly human relations (justice) that will inspire the energy (faith) that will both revive the ancient wisdoms and guide the creation of a new human society.

Raimon Panikkar

It is the cross-cultural
challenge of our times
that unless the barbarian, the
mleccha,
goy, infidel, nigger, kaffir,
foreigner, and stranger
are invited to be thou,
beyond those of my own clan,
tribe, race, church, or
ideology,
there is not much hope left for
the planet.

RAIMON PANIKKAR is
professor emeritus of the University
of California, Santa Barbara, and
is president of the "Vivarium",
Centre d'Estudis Interculturales in
Barcelona. He is the author of
many authoritative books focused
on the encounter of religions,
including *The Unknown Christ of
Hinduism* and *Faith and
Hermeneutics.*

There is something belligerent
inherent in our culture that makes us regard others as enemies, as
pagans, kaffirs, infidels, and such. It is not by chance that Western
civilization has developed its arsenal of weapons of mass destruction, immense both in its efficiency and in quantity.

Our preoccupation with the problems of peace, with the reduc-
tion of armaments, with eliminating violence in our streets, fails

routinely to face the underlying basic questions. No doubt our technocratic culture, its obsession with acceleration for acceleration's sake, has transgressed against all the natural rhythms of matter and of our minds. This has resulted in a society so unpeaceful that it makes achievement of peace in our time almost unthinkable. Peace, namely, does not entail the homogenization of everything, nor does it demand the denial of polarities. It demands participating in and contributing to the constitutive Rhythms of Reality. Discourse about peace has a tendency to weave idyllic dreams of paradisiacal bliss, as if the essence of the Eden story did not consist of paradise having been lost! Our destiny requires overcoming, not denying, the temporal strictures within which we are in danger of floundering. More than a thousand victims of war have died every day since the end of World War II. At this moment some twenty armed conflicts are raging, the number of refugees has reached millions, and so has that of street children, homeless, and starving people. We must not underestimate the level of dehumanization to which our species has fallen.

If some inner peace can be preserved, there is still a chance of human survival, for without inner peace the spectrum of individual and social plagues can be ascribed to this lack of inner peace without which there cannot be external peace, for it causes the competitiveness that always results in someone's defeat and triggers the longing for ruthless revenge. Is there another way of maintaining one's inner peace in our ecologically irresponsible human environment of violence and injustice than by consecrating oneself to alleviating suffering and injustice?

Life understood as the wisdom of Love and Compassion helps us to heal the split between inner and outer peace.

Peace cannot be "conquered" for oneself, nor can it be imposed on others. One cannot "fight" for peace as one can fight for one's rights or even for justice. To "fight" for peace is self-contradictory. We need a more "feminine" attitude toward receiving and transforming what we receive. In this context, *feminine* refers to compensating for what an exclusively male mentality has associated and enforced as positive values.

That victory never leads to peace is not a theoretical affirmation but an empirical statement: Some eight thousand peace treaties were signed over the millennia of human history. None of these has ever brought lasting peace. The defeated neither share nor enjoy the peace imposed by the victors.

No culture, no religion, no tradition can solve the world's problems in isolation. The key word for today is *pluralism*. There is no authentic spirituality which ignores the real world. Humankind should by now have learned the lessons of history, should have begun at last to contemplate the plausibility of a universal humanness that is transhistorical. Not only is our time ripe for such an anthropological mutation; it is a matter of survival or extinction. In the past the religions all too often have brought inner peace to their followers while fighting external wars against the others. This incongruity is today so manifest that the self-understanding of the religions is beginning to change to a concern with bringing peace to humankind and to the planet, to understand "peace" as a symbol universal, "pluralistic" enough to incorporate it in their teachings.

Forgiveness, reconciliation, ongoing dialogue, lead to peace, a peace that is a way forward, not backward, for any return to a status-quo ante is a pipe dream. In order to forgive, to dialogue, to establish reconciliation one needs a strength beyond the mechanical order of action and reaction. One needs the Holy Spirit, *karuna*, *charis*, and love realized as being the pillars of the universe.

To save humanity we have to become Human.

Ram Dass

RAM DASS was born in 1931 as Richard Alpert. In the 1960s he worked at Harvard University doing research into human consciousness, and he has continued that research for more than thirty-five years. His book *Be Here Now* has sold more than a million copies.

"I'm only human" is a response I recall using many times in my youth to explain why I couldn't fulfill all the expectations of the people around me. Probably that idea of being human derived from the mythology I grew up with (religious and secular) that portrayed humans in comparison to beings in the God realms and found humans to be weak, greedy, and rather stupid. Later, when I shed some of the myths that had guided my early life and became a social scientist (thus embracing a whole new set of myths), the term *human* came to stand for *Homo sapiens*, a species of primates with an evolved neocortex as the front-most layer of the brain that accounted for all our uniquely human attributes.

In the 1960s, while in my thirties, through personal experiences in consciousness and spirituality, and as a result of the grace of meeting great souls such as my teacher in India, I came to realize that a human is a far grander being than I had thought. These wise ones that I had the good fortune to meet, while rare, showed me the vast potential of human consciousness as something far more mysteriously fascinating than simply neocortical functioning. They showed me what it was to become fully human. Though their wisdom and compassion were great, these beings did not seem like gods to me. They were still "only human," though I now saw that term in a new light, no longer as an explanation for failure but rather as reassurance that what they had realized was available to me, as a fellow human being.

In the course of the past thirty years, spiritual practices have helped me (and tens of thousands of others) to expand awareness and in doing so to break out of the prison of separateness. This has involved me in the surrounding world in a new and far more intimate way. In so doing I, for one, have had to confront the fear of being overwhelmed by the suffering of my fellow beings and my impotence to do more than the tiniest things to alleviate their pain and the injustice under which so many live. Many times I found this situation unbearable. But, of course, it was only unbearable to whom I defined myself to be. As I surrendered that model of myself, I experienced an opening into a greater self that could embrace what is and could bear what must be borne.

In this new expanded self, appropriate compassionate action arose in my heart quite spontaneously out of the open engagement with suffering. No longer was it "their" suffering. Now it was "our" suffering, or, in some states of awareness in which one experiences the unity beyond the diversity, it was "my" suffering, and "my" compassion arising to meet it. Purely an international affair!

Once I found this deep well of compassion even within myself, I began to recognize it latent or manifest in so many others and came to see how often this vast internal reservoir of loving compassion was veiled from all of us by our fears. Humans can so easily get lost in the sea of ignorance in which the illusion of their own vulnerable separateness is seen as the only reality, and the fear that that identity evokes leads to behaviors of anger and greed, cynicism and violence, escapism, oppression, and cruelty. These behaviors, so obsessively portrayed by the media, lead to the breakdown of the very social systems, such as the family and community, on which civilization depends.

Our response to these aspects of our humanity need not be despair or a sense of hopelessness. Perhaps we are witnessing an evolution of consciousness, arising, like the Phoenix, from within the very crises and innovations of our times. Perhaps, for example, the technology which has given rise to the "information age," if used wisely, can help us to escape from our ethnic-socio-egocentrism and through dialogue awaken in us a perspectival vision—the ability to see situations from many different perspectives and thus from a more compassionate vantage point. Perhaps such technology, along with eco-crises and multinational commerce, both of which transcend national borders, can, if dealt with wisely, catalyze the expanded consciousness out of which generosity and compassion would arise spontaneously in our collective heart as a response to the barbarism of the day.

Seeing how civilization is rooted in the web of collective thought and seeing how quickly thoughts change, I am reassured that what we seek for humanity is intrinsic within it and always just one thought away. Each of us is the cocreator of the very defining thought. C. S. Lewis wrote: "You do not see the center, because it is all center." So I work on myself and do what I can. "What you do in response to the ocean of suffering may seem insignificant, but it is very important you do it," Gandhi consoles me.

Donella Meadows

To be human is to be born with an enormous package of potentials, for hatred and suspicion, for love and trust, for greed, generosity, passion, apathy— and a long list of other positive and negative traits. I guess all those traits can be found in many mixtures inside each of us. I sure can find them all in me.

DONELLA MEADOWS is a systems analyst, journalist, and organic farmer. She is an adjunct professor of environmental studies at Dartmouth College. She was coauthor of *Limits of Growth* and *Beyond the Limits*.

To be human is to be born into a world that pulls out and pushes back the potentials inside us. I push and pull back, trying to find or shape a part of the world (including other people) that supports my inborn potential. We do a dance, the world and I. Sometimes the world supports part of me. Sometimes it crushes part of me. Sometimes I learn something that seems to change me entirely—but more likely just brings out a part of me I didn't know was there.

Being human, I am blessed with remarkable organs of perception that bring millions of messages from the world—and I can be so dazzled by my own constant barrage of experience that I take it for the whole world. But I've learned, the hard way, that my experience isn't the world. It's only a tiny sample.

So I need other people, who have sampled other parts of the world. Together we can make a more complete picture. I need to report my piece of reality honestly, listen to others, and remember that the bit of truth I know is not anywhere near all the truth there is.

There's a part of me—it feels as if it's buried deep—that shines. It literally shines, or so it seems to me, with a warm and steady glow. It's where my deepest wisdom and best instincts come from. That part of me seems, in a way I can't explain (and I was trained as a scientist; I squirm at things I can't explain), to be simultaneously inside me and beyond me. It's connected to the whole universe. It's ancient, loving, noble. I think it's what other people mean when they use words like *conscience* or *soul* or *God*.

Most of the time I keep it well buried under a sludge of busyness, complaints, schemes, worries, fantasies, and fears.

I can only suppose that all of us have that glowing spot of wisdom within us. I think we differ greatly in our ability to contact it. Different inner potentials and different outer experiences must generate different amounts of sludge. And we live in cultures, created collectively by ourselves, that can encourage sludge—or encourage ready access to the inner shining.

Since I experience my culture and myself shaping each other in a dance, I find myself unable to put blame or credit for human actions fully on either the individual or the culture. I know from the nightly news that when dictators put guns in the hands of young men and women and tell them to shoot certain kinds of persons, a lot of those young women and young men—but not all—will shoot. If their culture had encouraged them from birth to be guided by their own internal nobility, most of them—but not all—would not shoot. I think so anyway. I've never known a culture like that.

The culture I live in powerfully encourages sludge and shooting. It does not lead people to experience the shining place inside themselves. My sorrow about this is so deep that I can't begin to express it. I see the news, the ads, the politics, the pop songs, the malls, the movies, the dope, the blight, the organized injustice, and I weep inside.

What kind of dance can I do with a culture that loads me with sludge and does not recognize my inner shine? All I can think to do is to tune into whatever I can know of the light and love of the universe, without denying the existence of my faults and failures. I guess both are intrinsic parts of my humanity. I can respect myself and others for the moments of nobility we do manage to produce out of the incredible mix of potential and experience, shine and sludge, that we carry around with us. We do, with astonishing frequency, produce moments of nobility. Our culture just doesn't choose to feature them on the nightly news.

I weep for the culture, but when I think about who I am, who we all are, we humans, I have to laugh—laugh as I would laugh at a child or a puppy, bumbling and self-centered, a still-unrealized being, but wonderfully endearing, infinitely lovable, full of potential.

Seyyed Hossein Nasr

SEYYED HOSSEIN NASR, a distinguished professor at the George Washington University, is one of the foremost Islamic scholars in the United States.

The humanity of the human state cannot be simply and solely or even primarily defined in relation to or determined by the biological world of which we are a part nor the society in which we live and which affects us in so many external ways. Man, by whom I mean not the male but the human species, was created in the "image" of God, to use Islamic as well as Jewish and Christian language, while remembering the differences in the meaning of *image* in each of these traditions.

Deep down within our being, beyond all the accidents and contingencies of time and space, we still bear this divine imprint upon our soul, and it is this divine imprint, and not any biological, social, or psychological determination or conditioning, that determines our humanity. The reason in fact that five hundred years after the rise of Renaissance humanism one has to pose today the question "What does it mean to be human?" is that since that time most of modern Western thought has sought to define human beings by means of something which has stood below the human. By seeking to reject the Divine Norm and be merely human, modern man has fallen below the human to the infrahuman, and now, five centuries later, we have to pose the question at hand concerning the nature of being human. Traditional civilizations, whether Confucian, Hindu, Christian, or Islamic, never spoke about humanism but also had no doubt as to what it meant to be human and created societies in which the highest human qualities were reflected, as were, of course, inevitable human frailties.

To be human means first of all to possess an intelligence which can know the truth and falsehood, beauty and ugliness, goodness and evil. It means to be capable of reaching certitude, to know in an absolute sense, and finally to know the Absolute as such and relativity as relativity in light of the Absolute. It also means to have the free will to choose and, more specifically, the will to choose the true, the real, the beautiful, and the good and to attach oneself to them. The human state implies the freedom of choice, hence moral responsibility. It is this freedom which proves in a blinding fashion the presence of the mark of the Divine, who is absolute Freedom as well as absolute Necessity, upon the human soul.

The grandeur of the human state is precisely the possession of this freedom of choice with all the opportunities and dangers that accompany it. It is the trust (al-amanah) which, according to the Quran, God offered to the heavens, the earth, and the mountains but they turned it down in fear of its consequences. Only man accepted this trust which presents him not only with the opportunity to journey beyond all becoming to the Divine Presence Itself but also with the risk of sinking below all creatures in his power of destruction and evil. The covenant (al-mithaq) made between God and man involves precisely the acceptance of God's lordship and our servitude and at the same time viceregency on earth. By virtue of this trust, we can play either the role of God's viceregents on earth to establish peace and justice among ourselves and in relation to the world of nature, or through delusion to seek to replace God with man, the kingdom of God with the kingdom of man, to play the role of gods on earth with power to wreak havoc upon God's creation and spread corruption upon the earth.

Besides the intelligence to know the truth and the will to cling to it and to choose the good, human beings also possess a soul which can become embellished by virtues that belong ultimately to God or to the spiritual world in traditions of a nontheistic character. Other creatures are what they are. Only man can be transformed by both virtue and vice. The character of malleability and the possibility of education in the vastest sense of the term, which includes of course spiritual training, is an essential aspect of human nature. A quartz crystal is always a quartz crystal with slight modifications and a dog is always a dog even after extensive training. But man can cover a vast range of existence which in principle covers the whole chain of being as this term was understood in traditional Western and Islamic philosophy. A human being can be a saint and a seer, a light unto the world, with goodness and charity which knows no bounds. He can also be so evil that no creature can be compared to him in the degree of destruction and subversion that he brings about.

The soul can only be trained by a reality above itself, by what is traditionally called the Spirit. All the goodness we observe in human beings is the result of what has been given to the soul from the spiritual world. As already mentioned, virtues on the highest level belong to God and we only participate in them. Those who deny God and the spirit and yet believe in the goodness of human nature are like a prodigal son who, while cursing his father, is living from his inheritance. Human nature is innately good because it was created by God, but it is not good in itself at its present state and moment of cosmic history, because that primordial nature has become so forgotten and covered over by so many layers of negligence and forgetfulness, which in Islam is considered as the major cause of all sin. To claim the goodness of humanity while denying the Good is to condemn human beings to the worst kinds of evil, as the history of the modern world has demonstrated so amply. Even for many Christians, how forgotten have become the words of Christ, who said, "Why callest thou me good; there is none good but one, that is, God." (Matthew 19:17) The great crisis of our day can in fact be reduced from a certain point of view to the attempt to claim the goodness of humanity while denying the very reality of the Good as such, to love the neighbor without loving God, to seek peace while turning away from that peace that "passeth all understanding."

Any humanism of a secularist nature which seeks to understand the meaning of being human in human terms alone is condemned to falling into the subhuman and finally into that reign of the machine and of quantity which smothers and strangulates the human itself. For human beings to seek to be merely human is to fall below the human, for as asserted by so many traditional sages, including St. Augustine, to be human is to seek to transcend and go beyond the merely human. This search for perfection and thirst for the Infinite and Absolute is inseparable from human nature; and when divorced from the goal for which it was created in us, namely, the Divine Reality which is the Infinite, the Absolute, and the Good or Perfect as such, this thirst manifests itself in the most destructive ways imaginable including quest for power and domination and a never-ending appetite for the possession of objects to fill the spiritual void at the center of the soul. Consumerism, which is destroying the natural environment, is an indirect proof of man's thirst and need for the Infinite.

To be human, then, means to exercise that intelligence given to us by the Ontological Principle that has determined our existence from on high to discern between truth and falsehood and good and evil. It means to exercise our will to choose truth over falsehood and goodness over evil, which means also choosing beauty over ugliness and ultimately Reality over the illusory. It also means embellishing the soul with those virtues which allow us to go beyond the boundaries of the ego that stifles the spirit within us and causes aggression against other creatures. To be virtuous means to cultivate humility, charity, and truthfulness along with all the other virtues such as patience, nobility, generosity, love, and sincerity that are related to them. It also means to practice these virtues firstly in relation to the Divine Principle and secondly in relation to all creatures including even those human beings who remain impervious to this imprint themselves or even deny it aggressively. But this embracing of all other human beings does not mean putting charity above the truth, for the rights of the truth are the highest of all rights and one cannot commit a sin against the Holy Ghost, to use a Christian concept, in the name of charity. Also to be truly human means to see the imprint of the Divine upon all other creatures and not to trample upon their rights in the name of the rights of human beings. It is this absolutization of the human state and its rights in modern Western thought, along with greed and avidity so evident in modern economic life, that is one of the major causes for the environmental crisis that now threatens human existence itself.

There is no possibility of a global bond between all human beings on the basis of a secular humanism. Human nature is too turbulent and unstable to be the foundation for unity of peoples and races of which there is so much talk today. The unity of the human species issues from two sources: the first is the inner and transcendent unity of the religious and revelations which through different forms but a single inner message have molded the soul and psyche of the different peoples of the world over the centuries and millennia. The second is that primordial substance of nature of the human species which has received different forms of the divine imprint over the ages and to which the Quran refers when it says that God has created humanity from a "single soul" (*nafs wahidah*). This inner and primordial nature is, however, not manifest or easily accessible in all human beings today and what we call simple human nature in everyday parlance must not be confused with it.

To bring about unity today and to even speak of what human

nature means in a manner that would be truly global and not provincial, we must turn to the inner teachings of various traditions concerning the human state. We shall then discover an incredible unity of doctrine beyond the bewildering variety of forms and concepts. One can in fact speak of an *anthropologia perennis* in the same way that one can speak of a *philosophia perennis* or *cosmologia perennis*. Once we discover these teachings so glibly forgotten in the modern world, we will no longer even have to ask what it means to be human. We will know with certitude that to be human is to be aware of the divine imprint upon the very substance of our being which defines us from on high and also reveals to us our responsibilities toward our Origin, other human beings, and the other creatures with whom we share our earthly abode. It means to be always aware of our Origin and End and of our vocation in this world in light of the alpha and the omega of our existence which determine our earthly existence but are themselves beyond the terrestrial.

To be human is to be aware of the Sacred and the Eternal. Our inner eye, identified by the Sufis with the "eye of the heart," was created to gaze upon the Divine. Our inner ear was meant to hear the eternal melodies of the heavens and our inner sense of smell was designed to experience the aromas of paradise. We are like a bridge between Heaven and earth, our inner faculties tuned to the abode of oneness and our external senses to the world of multiplicity. We were meant to act as a channel of grace from the One to the domain of the manifold, to be a source of light in the world while deriving this light from the Source of all light, to receive from Heaven and to disperse peace, harmony, compassion and justice upon the earth. To be human is to remain faithful to our role as the bridge between Heaven and earth and never forget the inner man and our inward "senses" turned to the Sacred and the Eternal. We must never allow the silent music of the spiritual world, to which our inner ear is still attuned, to become drowned out by the noise and cacophony of the external world. We cannot in fact bring goodness and justice into this world in an effective manner without remembering who we are inwardly and what our vocation is here on earth, for we are creatures living in time but created for eternity. We must love and serve others to the extent of our ability but we must do so while being always aware that the love of the neighbor is a consequence of the love of God and cannot replace the latter. We must always remember that there is no good without the Good and that our function as bride between Heaven and earth is precisely to bring the light of the Good into this world of imperfection and seek to create the peace which belongs ultimately to the heavenly abode, to the world of contention and strife that surrounds earthly human existence.

We can never cease to seek the supreme Goal for which we were created. We cannot break the vessel of our existence which we have not created ourselves. We do, however, have the freedom to fill this chalice during our lives here on earth with either a pungent poison which cannot cause but death and misery or the celestial nectar which brings about ecstasy and the paradisal joy for which we were created and which we can realize here on earth through truth and virtue and through prayer which awakens us to the truth and helps to sink the roots of virtue in our soul.

Having gazed upon the Face of the Friend in pre-eternity, how can I but be a witness to Him here below?

Gary MacEoin

Our society is dehumanizing rapidly. Social pulverization—driven by consumerism—destroys community, leaving isolated individuals who have been brainwashed. Politicians and advertisers join in pro-

GARY MacEOIN is an author and publicist. He is an expert on Vatican matters and the politics of Latin America.

claiming greed as the supreme virtue. Fear of our fellow humans is promoted to sell protective devices, from militarized living compounds and bullet-proof automobiles to assault rifles.

The gap worldwide between the few humans living at a human level and the many living below that level has widened and may be expected to widen further. The scientific slaughter of the Gulf War is praised, the 500,000 dead children, casualties of the continuing blockade of Iraq, counted an acceptable by-product. The institutionalization of barbarism, of torture in the interrogation of suspects, spreads apace. Convicted felons run for public office, and some of them win.

Violent crime escalates in the United States at three times the level of thirty years ago, with rape and aggravated assault topping the escalation. Youth and gang violence, especially drive-by shootings, have become part of city life. Robberies are four or five times more frequent than the average in fifteen other "advanced" Western countries. Homicides are three times more frequent in the United States than in Finland, which has the second-highest homicide rate worldwide. The global disparity in death by shooting is even more shocking: in a recent year, there were 10 killings in Australia, 22 in Sweden, 87 in Japan, 10,567 in the United States—statistics courtesy of the National Rifle Association.

Politicians decry the decay of "family values" but fail to note that our consumer society guarantees the destruction of the family by forcing both parents to work, offering the children a diet of TV that glorifies violence, presents the gun as the solver of every problem, and describes heaven as a glut of consumer goods.

In the face of all this, are there grounds for hope? I am continually sustained by the people I know—and the many I know about indirectly—who are committed to bringing our world to the level of perfection of which it is capable.

I think of Thomas Roberts, the puckish English Jesuit, for many years Archbishop of Bombay, who delighted in ridiculing the self-importance of the cardinals and bishops of the Roman Curia in his interventions in St. Peter's at the Second Vatican Council. A dedicated pacifist, he inspired the small antiwar group on the margin of the Council at which in 1963 I met Frederick Franck, staunch believer in Reverence for Life, hence in John XXIII, who exclaimed, "I love life!"

I have seen more of the world than most people. And wherever I have gone, I have been inspired by the emergence to historic visibility of peoples oppressed, ignored, and despoiled for hundreds of years: New Zealand's Maori, Australia's Aborigines, Canada's Inuit, and the Mayans of southern Mexico and Guatemala. Their new role as subjects of their own destiny was highlighted in the 1992 commemorations (no longer "celebrations"!) of the fifth centenary of the European invasion of the Americas.

Willis Harman

My own acquaintance with Reverence for Life came slowly, over many years. It seems incredible, looking back, that one could have such a strong resistance to what one most deeply desires. This acquaintance came in the form of the discovery of prayer.

WILLIS HARMAN was president of the Institute of Noetic Sciences in Sausalito, California, from 1978 until his death in 1997.

Like many people of my generation (I was born during World War I), I grew up with prayer being a foreign concept. Of course I had heard about prayer, but the prayers in church (on those extremely rare occasions when I attended) left me more bored than anything. The science I was learning in school gave no encouragement toward thinking there could possibly be anything to the supposed power of prayer. The prayer of gratitude struck me as particularly silly. It sounded like congratulating God on what a great job he did creating the universe.

When I was thirty-six I was tricked into going to a two-week retreat in the Northern California redwoods. I say "tricked" because if I had known what was likely to happen to me there I never would have set foot near the place. It had been represented to be a nonreligious discussion of the ethics and life principles of Jesus of Nazareth, without any talk of miracles. This was long before the era of sensitivity training and encounter groups, let alone EST and its many cousins. But here we were, spending long periods meditating, sharing with one another what we had felt deeply about, both positively and negatively, throughout our lives.

I found it all pleasurable and in some way fascinating. Toward the end I realized that I felt betrayed by the leader who had enticed me to enroll. He had not revealed that he believed there is something to the power of prayer, and I felt that someone with his education (he was a full professor at Stanford) ought to know that science had disproved that hypothesis long ago.

The last day I burst into tears when I was attempting to describe what I felt I had gotten from the seminar. I was aware that the sobbing had more to do with joy than with sadness, but I couldn't for the life of me give a good explanation of what lay behind it. It was as though some part of me was signaling that it was about time I got my life off dead center.

Clearly there were aspects of life they never told me about in school. Resolutely I set out to find out about those. As the decades went on (I am a slow learner) I had a series of experiences that filled my life with meaning. They centered around the concept of prayer.

It gradually dawned on me that how we see and experience ourselves and the world around us depends upon the beliefs we have internalized along the way. We are all culturally hypnotized from birth! It explained so much!

Now prayer had a meaning—prayer, as I now realize, as autosuggestion. If I suggest to myself, in a state of deep acceptance, that the world is full of wonder, or that I already have what will make me happy, it could really change things. It made sense.

But I kept hearing stories about concrete results coming from petitionary prayer—about real phenomena seemingly coming about through asking God for something. Meanwhile my own meditative experiences were going deeper, and the profound connectedness of everything was becoming something I really experienced. But if everything is connected to everything, why should it not be the case that if I imagine something, prolongedly and/or repeatedly, as vividly as possible and I repeat or hold that imagining that something might be manifested? There are no limits to what the Universe can manifest. Petitionary prayer made sense.

However, something about all that was troubling. Let's suppose it is true that if I choose to pray for something, that can influence that something's coming into being. But who is doing the choosing? If I am intimately connected to the Whole, do I really want what I think I want, or is that just the ego having its way? Don't I really want exactly what the Universe wants, since ultimately that is who I am? The prayer "Thy will be done" began to make more sense than anything else.

That conviction was amplified by a "near-near-death experience" at around sixty. I wasn't physically near death, but I was in a profound depression. For the first time I understood what people go through with psychological depression. This episode seemed to have to do with the deep realization—I felt it somewhere in the region of my stomach—that my life was approaching its end. It really felt like a death experience, and then one morning I walked up the hill to see the sunrise and it all lifted. Life was joyous again. But something was clear (at a deep feeling level) that had not been before. All the things that I had been taught all of my life were of value, clearly were of no value at all. In a few instants they would be gone. But one thing is of value—and only one. Alan Watts called it "the Supreme Identity"—the identification with the Divine.

And now another kind of prayer began to make sense. If I am really cocreator of the Universe, then the power of the prayer of gratitude is obvious. It is not just that by focusing on what is beautiful, and good, and true, and experiencing a deep feeling of profound gratitude, I changed the way I see the world. I actually change the world! It may be the most effective kind of service I can render.

I am now—statistically speaking—in the twilight of my life. The great adventure of death cannot be too far off. That fact in no way diminishes the delight of being out in nature, or playing with my great-grandchild, or enjoying the quiet comfort of a marriage that has lasted five and a half decades.

I could never have been persuaded, in my early years, that growing old can be thoroughly delightful. But in truth it is, every moment of it. To realize that at some deep level in ourselves we choose to age and die and watch the process with as much joy and satisfaction as a new father might delight in watching the birth of his child. It becomes more obvious each day that I am merely a part of the Whole.

Juliet Hollister

To be human is to belong to the species *Homo sapiens*, the occasionally upright mammal emerging from the caves. From being biologically human to being fully Human is the giant leap to the ability to perceive life and living beings in a brand-new way: the unprecedented grasp of a hand in deep empathy becomes possible, and spontaneous acts of kindness, of compassion, even of love—expressed in a myriad of ways.

JULIET HOLLISTER is the founder of the Temple of Understanding, a nonprofit educational organization to further communication among and about world religions. She has received the Eleanor Roosevelt and Albert Schweitzer Humanitarian Awards.

I see the fully Human as manifest in the Buddha, the Christ, a few millennia ago. In our time the Gandhis, Martin Luther Kings, Schweitzers continue to bear their torches in our darkness: astonishing manifestations of generically Human life and of reverence for it.

Trying to follow these torches, we fall flat on our faces again and again. And yet, once in a while their light penetrates the heart and, beyond the heart, the soul, and we are aware of being on the journey from having been born human to having become Human.

Mother Teresa

When I pick up a person from the street, hungry, I give him a plate of rice, a piece of bread. But a person who is shut out, who feels unwanted, unloved, terrified, the person who has been thrown out of society— that spiritual poverty is much harder to overcome.

Those who are materially poor can be very wonderful people. One evening we went out, and we picked up four people from the street. And one of them was in a most terrible condition. I told the Sisters, "You take care of the other three; I will take care of the one who looks worse." So I did for her all that my love can do. I put her in bed, and there was such a beautiful smile on her face. She took hold of my hand as she said these words only: "Thank you." And she died.

MOTHER TERESA was born Agnes Bojaxhiu in the former Yugoslavia in 1910. In 1950 she started the Congregation of the Missionaries of Charity in Calcutta, which has expanded to include 600 homes in 136 countries. Before her death in 1997, she was the recipient of many prestigious awards, including the Nobel Peace Prize.

I could not help but examine my conscience before her. And I asked, "What would I say if I were in her place?" And my answer was very simple. I would have tried to draw a little attention to myself. I would have said, "I am hungry; I am dying; I am cold; I am in pain," or something. But she gave me much more—she gave me her grateful love. And she died with a smile on her face.

Then there was the man we picked up from the drain, half-eaten by worms, and, after we brought him to the home, he only said, "I have lived like an animal in the street, but I am going to die as an angel, loved and cared for." Then, after we had removed all the worms from his body, all he said, with a big smile, was, "Sister, I am going home to God." And he died. It was so wonderful to see the greatness of the man who could speak like that without blaming anybody, without comparing anything. Like an angel—this is the greatness of people who are spiritually rich even when they are materially poor.

We are not social workers. We may be doing social work in the eyes of some people, but we must be contemplatives in the heart of the world. For we must bring that presence of God into your family. There is so much hatred, so much misery, and we with our prayer, with our sacrifice, are beginning at home. Love begins at home, and it is not how much we do but how much love we put into what we do.

If we are contemplatives in the heart of the world with all its problems, these problems can never discourage us. We must always remember what God tells us in Scripture: "Even if a mother could forget the child in her womb—something impossible, but even if she could forget—I will never forget you."

And so here I am talking with you. I want you to find the poor here, right in your own home, first. And begin love there. Be that good news to your own people first. And find out about your next-door neighbors. Do you know who they are?

I had the most extraordinary experience of love of neighbor with a Hindu family. A man came to our house and said, "Mother

Teresa, there is a family who have not eaten for so long. Do something." So I took some rice and went there immediately. And I saw the children—their eyes shining with hunger. I don't know if you have ever seen hunger. But I have seen it very often. And the mother of the family took the rice I gave her and went out. When she came back, I asked her, "Where did you go? What did you do?" and she gave me a very simple answer: "They are hungry also." What struck me was that she knew—and who are they? A Muslim family—and she knew. I didn't bring any more rice that evening because I wanted them, Hindus and Muslims, to enjoy the joy of sharing.

But there are those children, radiating joy, sharing the joy and peace with their mother because she had the love to give until it hurts. And you see this is where love begins—at home in the family.

Mary Palmer Smith

MARY PALMER SMITH is part of the New Community Corporation in Newark, New Jersey, where she has helped establish seven day-care centers.

I grew up in New Jersey's largest public housing project with one thousand five hundred other families, in clusters of thirteen-story buildings riddled with misery and ugliness. Elevators more often than not were out of order, so that we had to trudge up endless flights of dirty stairs. According to the federal government, mosquito screens were not needed above the seventh floor as mosquitoes were not supposed to fly at higher altitudes! We lived on the eleventh floor. My children were eaten alive in summer, as they froze in winter, for heat and hot water were off more often than on. It was not a human habitat. It was not even a slum.

After the Newark riots in the summer of 1967, fueled by long-simmering racial tensions, the city deteriorated further. Buildings began to decay, people stopped cleaning up, and when suburbanites returned on a visit they said, "I lived here once, but look how bad it is now." The owners were still responsible for building maintenance, but they preferred to blame us poor black tenants for the general deterioration. Jobs dried up locally, and lack of mass transportation prevented people from commuting to where some work was available.

Our neighborhood was faced with all the problems of overcrowded schools, ever-increasing street crime, and a lack of police to curb it. I got insight into the attitudes of my fellow residents in public housing and began to organize them. They were receptive and we started our fight for improved living conditions. At one point we marshaled one thousand five hundred of us to attend a city council meeting. I became involved with the New Community Corporation and its founder, Monsignor William Linder, in 1966 and with Operation Understanding, an early civil rights movement in Newark, from which the remarkable group of women known as Operation Housewives evolved, when some twenty urban and suburban women got together and dedicated themselves to a fuller understanding of the views, hopes, and aspirations of inner city people, black women in particular. I chaired the group.

Each month we learned more about one another. We drank coffee together and honestly exchanged our often widely divergent points of view and what we desired most: the best possible education for our children, jobs that would enable us to support our families, safe, clean neighborhoods. Speaking engagements led me farther into the suburbs, where I explained the plight of the inner city and especially the lack of jobs for urban women. Even if it existed elsewhere, day care for children under age two and a half was not to be found in Newark, in fact nowhere in New Jersey.

Soon Operation Housewives started a thrift shop to raise enough money to start our first Babyland Nursery in August 1969, in a seven-room apartment in the very housing project I once lived in. It was quite beautiful, bright and cheerful with new furniture, equal to any child-care center I had visited with my suburban friends. Nothing in it was sloppy or inferior; both groups of women saw to that. My new suburban friends encouraged their husbands to volunteer services for our cause. Lawyers, doctors, contractors, teachers, businessmen rolled up their sleeves to help install carpeting, paint, renovate, offer legal advice and proposals, even medical care for the babies. We were humans together. A strong bond was forged between the less fortunate members of society and the more privileged ones who saw and understood the needs of the inner city and responded to it in warm, sensitive ways.

Today we continue our networking relationship with Monsignor Linder and New Community Corporation. We have become Babyland Family Services, one of the largest day-care organizations in the country, providing quality child-care services at all seven centers. One of these is an HIV center for HIV-infected children. We also run two twenty-four-hour shelters, one for victims of domestic violence, the other for foster care for siblings. Moreover we operate an after-school and summer enrichment program. We have 220 employees, serve nearly 800 children and 1,000 families a year in a city where there are still too few receiving help from those, all too few, who understand what it means to be human.

After twenty-eight years of working with human beings I have come to the conclusion that being human consists in an openness to others, in being clearly aware of common needs, and in working together on solving the problems and changing the circumstances that caused these problems, to have true reverence for the living reality of the other person.

Georg Feuerstein

I look around me, and what I see is an unprecedented socio-cultural chaos that rips my heart. What has humanity come to? Why this rampant disregard for all that is good and noble? Where did we learn to become so obsessed with reducing ourselves to cosmic dust? Why do we teach our children hate, disrespect, and,

GEORG FEUERSTEIN, Ph.D., is director of the Yoga Research Center and author of well over twenty books, including the award-winning *Shambala Encyclopaedia of Yoga*, *Structures of Consciousness*, and *Lucid Waking*.

above all, sheer indifference? How can anyone imagine survival is possible in our state of spiritual and moral anorexia?

I realize that I am an integral part of the chaos of this civilization. So I remind myself that even chaos is patterned, and I look more closely, more patiently. And what I see is complexity rather than chaos—a complexity that is at a cusp of crisis. I see my own complexity and understand that the crisis is as much within me as it is external to myself. My confusion is the confusion of all my fellow humans; their suffering is my own. I cannot divorce myself from the nexus of history. I am shaped by the thoughts and actions of others, and my own thoughts and actions codetermine their lives and thus our collective existence.

Only in my awareness can I rise above the threads that tie me to the past, present, and future of our species. That is the decisive point: the self-transcending power of awareness. And in that feat of awareness, I remind myself that every crisis is a moment of birth and that most births are *not* stillbirths but bring viable life into the world. In that moment of recognition, my hope is restored. I emerge from the tunnel into which our civilization has driven itself and breathe the sunny air of a new vision and destiny.

At this terminal hour, we must all win through to such understanding and hope, look clearly into ourselves and look around us lucidly, and be ready to perceive the weave of forces and counterforces that have pushed and pulled our species to its present point of crisis. In doing so, we would do well to exercise tolerance, patience, and compassion toward ourselves and others, though without committing the now-popular error of equalizing all values and leveling all differences. For there is right and wrong, viable and unviable. Therefore, discernment is essential. And discernment is a function of wisdom, and wisdom is the obverse of love, and love is what arises when we are at peace in our crystalline awareness. Then, and only then, can there be appropriate, balanced, benign, and effective action.

I wish and pray that many will find their way to this great awareness. I believe this is the only doorway to a future free from the kind of inhumanity of which only broken human beings bereft of wisdom and hope are capable.

Carman Moore

My first language is Music. When I think of what it means to be human at its most perfect and what it's like to speak Human, I think of music. I think of the language that cannot lie, regardless of what lyrics may be forced upon it. I think of a language that both heart

CARMAN MOORE is an African-American composer whose works have been performed at the Cathedral of St. John the Divine in New York, where he is conductor of the Children's Choir.

and head—left brain and right brain—Yin side and Yang side can all speak and comprehend with perfect, simultaneous, and equal clarity. Being human in this model/metaphor reminds one of what wonderful creations we can be, since music seen as that elemental force totally created from vibrations and the receiver's perception is nothing short of pure wonder. Variations on vibration form, pitch, rhythm, sonic color, melody, harmony, and even light. Perceiving those variations can make us respond with laughter, tears, knowing smiles, confusion, disgust, fascination, or myriad other expressions of the senses—new each time and nameless, unless, of course, we have learned to block out and rewire our feelings so that very few signals are allowed through without an interim step of left-brain scrutiny and labeling. This last represents the human in a state of emotional illness and fear—a state that has been upon us conspicuously in this century, separating us from certainty about God's love and the perfection of Tao. Through this self-rewiring of the natural, the human race has been, no doubt, trying to make doubly sure that others won't take advantage of us, that we'll always have plenty to eat and drink, plenty of loves and lovers, and as much excess wealth as possible, just in case. Let's see, we'll kill off any possible threats before they even dream of killing us, adapt a macho swagger so nobody and nothing will mess with us. Hey, we might live forever.

Whereas, in our music-loving state, in order to perceive all the music, we must surrender totally, letting the vibrations have their way with us; respond with defenseless honesty, chancing that we might find ourselves singing along or falling in love, feeling strange, or dancing ourselves to death, or entering a state of constant change bordering on Enlightenment. Dangerous, to be sure, but just as natural as the way any tree or bird lives.

Rewired, we find it natural to fear (as have the Nazis, Soviets, and Khmer Rouge) the possibility that the natural power of music and the arts might act to spur imaginative, fearless, clear thoughts and, with that, revolution. They've got a point there. If some regime seeks to keep people in disharmony with each other, out of step with themselves as individuals, used to stupidity and illogical, afraid to take any kind of solo turn, afraid of new forms, afraid of outbursts of public gentleness or human compassion . . . music could ruin everything.

Sometimes it feels to me as if everything I've learned that is advanced and beautiful either can be traced to music, is correlative with music, or feels great accompanied by music. Humans, if we want to survive, and certainly if we want to survive in beauty, power, and enlightenment, let us teach and never stop teaching and sharing all our music. When I feel what it feels like to be really human, I hear music.

Huston Smith

When my wife, Kendra, took our two-year-old grandson to the neighborhood playground recently, two children of Oriental extraction were already on the swings and slides—a girl of about eight and her brother, around five. After the barest preliminaries, the girl asked Kendra, "What are we?" "Vietnamese?" Kendra ventured.

HUSTON SMITH is Thomas J. Watson Professor of Religion and Distinguished Adjunct Professor of Philosophy, Emeritus, Syracuse University. His eight books include *The World's Religions, Forgotten Truth* and *Beyond the Post-Modern World*.

"No." "Filipino?" "No," with a touch of irritation entering. When Kendra proposed a third lineage the irritation exploded. *"No!* What *are* we?" Sensing that she was on the wrong track, Kendra decided that if she knew the answer she might better understand the question, so she gave up and asked, "What are you?"

"We are brother and sister," the girl replied emphatically, "so we love each other. And our grandmother tells us that if we love her, when we are grandparents our grandchildren will love us."

Out of the mouths of babes!—the girl had it *exactly* right. Not "who are we?," which points toward differences, but "what are we?" What is our nature, our human essence? And her answer was equally on the mark. Our essence is relatedness ("we are brother and sister"), and our primary relationship is that of love.

Perhaps it requires the innocence of childhood—a childhood shaped by traditional elders, moreover—to remind modernity of what the world's great wisdom traditions have unanimously claimed from the start: namely that, in Mencius' terse formulation, "Man is by nature good." Judaism and Christianity tell us that we were made in God's image, and Allah announces explicitly in the Koran that "We made man in the best stature" (95:4). In the South Asian family of religions, the individual soul is foundationally the Buddha-nature or Atman; and in the East Asian tradition it is the Uncarved Block whose wholeness antedates the wounds that society has inflicted on it.

This noble, traditional view of human nature contrasts sharply with the image of ourselves that science and modern psychology present us with. Frithjof Schuon calls our current image "pitiable"; and Saul Bellow, while more restrained, acknowledges in his Nobel Laureate Lecture that "we do not think well of ourselves; we do not think amply about what we are." Freud's view of human nature comes as close to a coherent view as we have today, and it is avowedly pessimistic. In the words of a poet, Czeslaw Milosz:

We used to see ourselves as handsome and noble
Yet later in our place an ugly toad—
Half-opens its thick eyelid
And one sees clearly: "That's me."

I do not find anything in what we objectively know that requires this diminished view of ourselves, but before I get to that I want to point to the toll this view is taking, for it is not easy to get out of mental ruts and our rut is a deep one. Unless we see where it is taking us, we are not likely to make the effort that will be needed to extricate ourselves from it.

Violence seems to be increasing. It's always been around, of course (Hegel called history a butcher's block), but from vandalism to random shootings, senseless, unprovoked violence at least, seems to be on the rise. Many causes conspire: erosion of the primary community, more "efficient" weapons, and the routinization if not glorification of violence by the media. But the ingredient I want to focus on is our reduced self-image.

There is nothing that the public at large—parents, teachers, and correctional officers in their number—would more like to learn from psychologists than what makes for behavior change. Thus far researchers haven't gotten very far with the question, but heading their provisional answers is a changed self-image. For people act out who they take themselves to be.

Here is where the question of human nature jumps to importance, for the nobler we imagine ourselves, the better we are likely to behave. It's quite simple, really. The better we feel about ourselves, the better we feel about others, and this leads us to treat them better. And to perform better generally. This is the conclusion of Robert Rosenthal's "Pygmalion in the Classroom" experiment which showed that pupils whose teachers thought they were intelligent came to believe that they were intelligent; which belief enabled them to perform more intelligently—their grades improved. Regardless of how much he felt he needed to cram, one of my college roommates always devoted the last half-hour before an examination to taking a shower and donning a white shirt. It jacked up his self-respect, he said.

Psychology stops with what that paragraph reports, but religions don't. They add creation myths—accounts of how people got here. And it is not difficult to see why they do so; for where people position themselves on the scale of self-esteem depends (more than on any other factor) on how they think they arrived—the ancestry they posit for themselves. Which posit (as we just noted) affects their behavior; this is the only way we can make sense of Rabbi Ben-Azzai's choice of "This is the book of the generations of Adam" (which is to say, the book that chronicles the human ancestry) as the most important book in the Torah. He placed it ahead of Rabbi Akiba's more celebrated choice—"Thou shalt love thy neighbor as thyself" because in Hebrew, Adam means man, and it is the realization that human beings were divinely created that *prompts* people to love their neighbors. To believe that one is descended from noble stock is to assume that one is made of noble stuff, which in turn disposes one to behave nobly, though of course it doesn't guarantee such behavior. Something like generational rub-off occurs, for where there is noble ancestry there are noble role models and shoddy conduct cannot be blamed on happenstance or shoddy genes.

When we add to the foregoing considerations Marshall Sahlins's anthropological observation that "we are the only people who think themselves risen from savages; everyone else believes they descended from gods," we have the gist of the point I have been trying to make; namely that the decline in our view of human nature is a serious matter. This lends urgency to the question of whether we are bound to that view. Do we know things our forebears didn't that force us to stay with the low view of human nature that currently hobbles us, or did we stumble into that view through mistakes?

Having argued the case for the latter alternatives in my *Forgotten Truth* and *Beyond the Post-Modern Mind*, I can content myself here with what bears directly on the issue at hand. Darwin paved the way for our current view, Freud rounded it off, and both were wrong—not about everything, but in the burden of their theses. Both will be around for a while, for the holds they have on our minds are strong. But as "isms," their grips will gradually relax.

To start with Darwinism: In describing *what* happened in life's ascent, evolution is solidly in place. But as a theory that claims to have discovered *how* that ascent took place—through naturalistic processes only—Darwinism lards its empirical findings with philosophical assumptions that turn it into an ideology; Philip Johnson's 1991 *Darwin on Trial* is right on that point. Darwinism will (and should) continue as science's working hypothesis on its subject, but its claim to providing the key to the puzzle is losing its hold on unbiased minds, because (after several centuries of uncertainty) we are coming to realize that the momentous, metaphysical issues regarding human existence cannot be answered within science's framework only. Even within science, Darwinism is slipping. In-house loyalty works to keep that quiet, but periodically the word leaks out. A recent instance: Normally, the *Scientific American* allots about a single column to the books it reviews; but when Johnson's just-cited book took Darwinism to task for its illegitimate hold on our thinking, the magazine reached for its biggest gun, Stephen Jay Gould, and gave him eight columns to debunk it as a bad book. Eight times a book's normal space for a *bad* book? The scientific community felt threatened.

As for Freud, disillusionment with his theories has been mounting since the seventies, but Frederick Crews brought it to a head in his 1993–1995 series of articles and exchanges in *The New York Review of Books* which (in expanded form) that magazine has published under the title *The Memory Wars*. More exhaustively, and in tandem with that book, the first 250 pages of Richard Webster's *Why Freud Was Wrong* (Basic Books, 1995) traces the way in which, burdened by his mother's doting expectations for her son, which brooked no criticisms, Freud allowed his messianic dreams to shape the "science" he created. Falling under the spell of his self-image as a charismatic theorist, he plunged into a labyrinth of error that blinded him to the fact that his sexual theories were religious doctrines in disguise, preserved from attacks from science only because he presented them as science. P. B. Medawar called psychoanalysis the hoax of our century, and fifty psychologists, historians, and other intellectual leaders—including Oliver Sachs and Gloria

Steinem—have signed a petition protesting the Library of Congress's projected exhibition on Freud on grounds it would support his dubious ideas.

It will take a decade or two to reverse a century's blunders concerning human nature, but we can be encouraged, not only by the collapse of the mainstays of those blunders, but by affirmative evidence that is emerging in science itself. Countering Freud's contention that lust and aggression are life's dynamos, experiments with macaque monkeys show that 87 percent would rather go hungry, some for as long as two weeks, rather than administer electrical shocks to their companions.

As for human beings, most psychologists have now dropped Freud's theory of innate drives. Their tendency is to replace it with a blank slate, but Ian Suttie (whose *Origins of Love and Hate* is one of the best-kept secrets of twentieth-century psychology, despite the fact that it influenced object relations theory via John Bowlby) posited an innate tendency for altruistic love. Suttie accepted the psychologists' notion that we shove thoughts and feelings that make us anxious into the unconscious, but he was convinced that the major human repression is not of sexual or aggressive impulses, but instead a repression of affection and openness. It is those, in his view, that are our original endowments, and it is their repression that adds up to the collective taboo on tenderness in our culture.

The chapter on "The Roots of Empathy" in Daniel Goleman's current best-seller, *Emotional Intelligence*, reports on ways in which this line of thought is being carried forward, but I have exhausted the space that was allotted me and will close with a fragment of a poem by Rumi that pretty much sums up my thesis.

If you could only see your beauty,
    for you are greater than the sun.
Why are you withered and shriveled in this prison of dust?
A basketful of bread sits on your head
    but you beg for crusts from door to door.

You are more precious than both heaven and earth.
You know not your own worth.
Sell not yourself at a little price,
    being so precious in the eyes of God.

Amanda Bernal-Carlo

AMANDA BERNAL-CARLO is a Colombian-born scholar of ecology and medicinal plants. She is an assistant professor on the faculty of Hostos Community College in New York.

When I was five years old I met Teofilo, an old man who lived in our small Colombian town. He was known as the *bobo del pueblo*, the village fool. He used to eke out a living doing simple little jobs. To the grown-ups he was just a fool, a dunce. To us children he was a playmate. The grown-ups did not suspect that behind the façade of the *bobo* there were hidden treasures of wisdom, insights into human nature, not learned from books—he was illiterate—but from long years of living his simple life with eyes and heart wide open. And so this humblest of human beings—this Zen fool—taught me in words a five-year-old could grasp that everything that is alive is important, is a magical event, and that the deepest sense of being alive lies in feelings of kinship with other beings, with the living and even the nonliving world.

Later I was to discover that my own feelings of kinship with all life, à la Teofilo, were also a part of the life practice of native peoples, that there survives in their souls the oneness of life that sages of all races and all faiths have taught to be an indispensable ingredient to any viable human community.

Traveling in the remote and inaccessible Sierra Nevada de Santa Marta of Colombia, I learned about the deeper sense of oneness of life that the dwellers of the Sierra, the Kogi Indians, are carrying in their hearts. These, our companions on earth, called us the younger brothers, because of our foolish ways to see and treat the world we share with them, especially the Sierra that they consider the Heart of the world. One day, so spoke the mamas—the wise priests and shamans of the Kogi:

Before the younger brother came, there was forest all the way down to the ocean, and there were many older brothers in the Sierra and around it. They did not cut the trees so that no diseases came, and the water could nourish itself, the trees could nourish themselves with the mist of the clouds.

The older brother, the trees, and the water respected one another as the trees respected the water, as we respected the trees, and the water respected us. We all respected one another equally. We respected one another by not making aqueducts and pipelines, by not throwing trash around or urinating in the ravines.

The trees were sons of Kalashe. Before younger brother there was Kalashe. When a tree was cut a foot of Kalashe was hurt; when he lay down it hurt, but when he got up the trees elevated again. One day Kalashe was killed. Knowing this history, the elder brother did not cut trees, so that thousands of people could live in many parts of the Sierra. They ate fish, game, and fruits. There were all kinds of game and fruits.

Before there was stone machete and so not the forest nor the land became sick. When younger brother came he brought us machete and ax, and cutting with these instruments sickness came. When the sap came out from the trees, then appeared diarrhea and vomiting of the blood.

But the younger brother told us that if you do not have a farm, if you did not grow cattle you are not a señor; you would be nothing but a savage. And so everybody began to cut down the forest, buy cattle, and start farms. That is why today it is so very difficult to retrieve the things we lost and why we are attacked by disease, hunger. The valley gets destroyed; the river dries out.

When the Heart gets sick everything and everybody gets sick; that is why you cannot cut trees at the foot of the Sierra. What does the younger brother think? Does he or does he not have a heart? Why does he not leave the forest alone so that our grandchildren can also enjoy it? All this because there is not enough money. But how did the ancients live?

The ancients knew that when there is ill-talk, conflict, violence, Serankua will send us punishment for disrespecting and the people will die. That is why we, the older brothers, do not want to have much money, or cars or cows. We need support to recover our traditions, our laws, and discover the true way because we do not want to suffer an eternal punishment when we die where Heisei is.

Now we have money. But what good will it do? We cannot allow the Heart to become weak and die. The Sierra is calling us to take care of it.

In the wisdom of the Kogi, I recognize the precepts that are at the core of the teachings of the Christ and the Buddha and that are mirrored at our deepest self, that reverence and compassion, that responsibility for all that lives, are the only safeguards of my children's future and that of their children, generation after generation.

Monsignor William Linder

It was the winter of 1963. I was a newly ordained priest just a few months into my first assignment at a parish in the Central Ward of Newark. I had been asked to bring food to an impoverished mother and child living in a decrepit building. The unheated apartment was freezing. A child deathly ill with pneumonia was lying motion-

MONSIGNOR WILLIAM LINDER founded the New Community Corporation in Newark, New Jersey, in the years following the race riots in that city. His work includes an exemplary community center and day-care centers. (This essay first appeared in 1995.)

less in a crib covered with wire mesh to protect it against rats.

When I returned two days later with more food, the child had died. I was stunned and frustrated, for although I could bring them some food, I had been unable to provide the medical help, the warm home they needed. I had cared but had failed. The senseless loss of this fragile life proved to be a catalyst in my own life, forcing me to reflect on the evil forces that had been brought to bear on this innocent victim of one of society's most pervasive pathologies.

This tiny human being was killed by racial hatred and contempt.

For thirty-two years now I have experienced this evil targeting of a people who have come to mean so much to me, the public policies which blame the victims of poverty. I witness the ever-increasing class distinctions created by the self-righteous, who declare that those born in poverty are poor because of their own choosing. I worry about a country that envisions the future as happening in the suburbs, letting the urban centers die, the places which historically have assisted millions of immigrants to become assimilated into America and have served as its cultural incubators.

The death of that infant became for me a symbol of this barbaric century. Think of the staggering numbers who died in World War I, World War II, the Korean and Vietnam Wars. Reflect on the 6 million Jews and half-million Gypsies who were murdered in the Holocaust. Today's news is filled with the atrocities in Bosnia, the ethnic wars in Africa, and the political violence of Southeast Asia.

As an example of how life is devalued, historians state casually that they are not certain whether the correct number is 15 million or 20 million human beings who died in Siberian concentration camps under Stalin.

Scientific advances, which could make a human environment possible, have given us a limitless capacity to destroy life. Technology has brought instant death in war to more humans in this twentieth century than ever before. The indirect destruction of human life through the abuse of the environment has made this into a century of death.

We frantically seek for Meaning as if our ancestors in every culture had not understood the why of their existence. It seems that the more "primitive" the culture (*simple* is a better word), the deeper the understanding of the meaning of life. Educated as we are, we seem to understand less the more we learn.

We have forgotten the importance of simple expressions of love which the children in our day-care centers show toward a visitor who becomes their instant new friend. We miss the kindness of the expression in the other's eyes; we ignore the symbolism of the simplest gifts. The word *love* has been abused until it has lost its meaning except perhaps in its religious context. My favorite Dostoyevski novel, *The Idiot*, whom I believe to represent Christ, could never be made into a television drama because it doesn't fit a culture which ignores that what we really have to share is life itself. Tolstoy's fictional peasants did not study philosophy, and yet they did grasp the meaning of life.

When the demands of my work and the negativism of our day start to overwhelm me, I flee to one of our "Babylands," our infant and toddler day-care centers, for here I can appreciate the gift of life; here one can always count on a hug. The loving acceptance by children never fails to improve my worst moods.

Often I reflect on the many wonderful people I have had the honor to associate with despite the devastating social issues of our time, as for instance the plague of AIDS—especially among small children—that challenges the human spirit and is one to which people respond heroically. Dr. Jim has dedicated his professional career to HIV-positive children. He and his nurse-associate in a nearby urban hospital provide not only excellent care but a loving environment in their pediatric AIDS unit. Terry and Faye operate an AIDS hospice for infants and toddlers. This husband-and-wife team, assisted by others, offers the unconditional love which every child should experience. Our own Gina and Sister Suzie head a day-care center for infants and toddlers with AIDS. They demonstrate that the human spirit is still capable of rising to the challenge. Because of the loving attention these children receive, they have a more normal childhood and their short life expectancy is doubled.

It is one thing for a priest to experience death in almost daily visits to the hospital, but it is a different thing to witness the senseless death of an innocent infant because of hatred. The realization of my limitations gave birth to the concept of New Community. What I could not accomplish alone I could do with others, enlisting the help of the very people who needed the opportunity for a better life. They might have lacked material things, but they proved they did not lack the Spirit.

Thus the death of that baby over thirty years ago taught me to reflect on the principles of urban community development which would constitute the essential elements of the community experiment and the model known as the New Community Corporation of Newark, New Jersey.

Alexander Eliot

What does it mean to be human? I'm not sure because I haven't got there yet. Still, in the course of a lifelong quest I've met at least a dozen people who qualify. Here is one such:

ALEXANDER ELIOT is a pilgrim mythologist, contemplative traveler, and author of *The Timeless Myths, The Global Myths,* and *The Universal Myths,* among others.

A fisherman of Mount Athos in Greece told me about Karoulia. It lies beneath a tiny anchorage in a curtain of cliffs near the Holy Mountain's southernmost tip. Monks who have grown extremely old and sanctified retire to Karoulia, the fisherman said, and live on the ledges along the cliff.

"Is anyone there now?" I asked.

"Of course. I'll run you down in my boat if you like. You may even see him."

"Who?"

"Him. Simon. A very holy fellow."

The next morning was calm, serene. The fisherman and I dropped down the coast in his squat little boat, past Dionysicu. We anchored without difficulty in under the cliff. Footholds had been

109

cut in the rock. Chains hung from spikes driven in beside the steps. The chains and steps together made a zigzag pattern overhead. One wire cut straight down across them to the anchorage, like a sword stroke. I asked the fisherman what that was for.

"The holy Simon," he said, "sends his basket down on that wire. When we come by this way we put something into the basket for him to eat. It's not here today, though. That means he's fasting."

"Would it be all right for me to disturb him at such a time?"

The fisherman shrugged: "If those chains will hold you, it is as God wills."

So I started climbing up alone, hanging onto the chains. It was hard going. After a while I thought fatigue and vertigo would do me in. I reached the point of no return. I knew I lacked the strength to about-face and climb all the way down again, so I pressed on. I reached a broad ledge, finally, and pulled myself up onto it. There I lay gasping like a landed fish, prone, profoundly uncurious, staining the rock with sweat. Then I sensed that someone stood over me; his shadow felt cool across my shoulders. I turned onto my back. Sparkling-eyed, erect, nearly toothless, and like a skeleton, Simon spread his arms wide.

"*Oriste!*" he said, meaning, "Welcome! What can I do for you?" The Greek word also connotes the horizon, appropriately enough.

Simon welcomed me to a fresh-made world. The sea, the sun, the rock, the man himself, seemed to have stepped through to existence a moment before. They were newborn; I was the old one. Dumbly I rose. The hermit took my hand and led me along the ledge to a little garden of earth which he had inserted in a lip of rock. He showed his few rows of struggling, growing greenery. I made no comment. They were tomato plants, I imagine, as I look back. Simon drew me on into a tiny rock chapel which he had built. The hermit invited me to pray, and afterward he brought me into his cave cell. It was a clean, dim, tidy room. He made me sit, like an honored guest, in the one chair. I longed to question him, yet not one question came to mind. I simply could not speak to such a man.

I was afraid that if I said a word some subtle vermin visible to him would pop out of my mouth. Yet even that, I think, would not have surprised or upset Simon. He took my silence with attentive calm. Somewhere he found a caramel candy. This he put by itself on a saucer and ceremoniously offered to me.

I hesitated, I suppose, before accepting the candy. Then as I raised it to my lips a dreary sense of the practical world returned to me. I had not thought to bring a gift for the hermit. His bones showed; they seemed ready to break through the parchment skin. He needed nourishment, as I myself did not. Thinking these things, I palmed the caramel. Surreptitiously I slipped it underneath the saucer for him to find later. Then I got up, bowed as low as I could, and hurried out, away, over the ledge. I swung down the long chains to the anchorage.

The sun was just setting when I arrived. The fisherman sprawled on his boat deck, asleep. I stripped off my clothes and stepped into the pink and crystal water. I floated out around the boat, turned on my back, and gazed up at the sky. A distant hum came down to me. It grew into a kind of shriek, descending swiftly, as if to attack! But I could see nothing coming. Numb with terror, I let myself sink. I swam underwater into the shadow of the boat. There I surfaced and looked up warily. The wire which cut diagonally down across the cliff was vibrating. A string hung loosely curled along the wire. That, I felt sure, had not been there before. And then I realized what must have occurred. Simon had let his basket slide noisily down the wire, on purpose. Yes, there lay the basket. It was a high-sided pannier of straw, leaning against the iron spike to which the wire was anchored. Splashing ashore, I peered inside. My candy had come back! I put the caramel straight into my mouth. And like a child once more I tasted its burnt sugar elixir right down to my toes.

Never before in this life, possibly, had my poor spirit taken nourishment. I stood dripping upon the shore of time, and Simon waved to me from eternity.

James Parks Morton

JAMES PARKS MORTON, dean emeritus of the Cathedral of St. John the Divine in New York, is a social and interfaith activist whose work has come to be identified with humanitarian issues as they relate to the spiritual lives of people of all cultures and religions.

In the last three decades, we have gone through a tremendous revision of what it means to be a human being. We are still in the middle of it, so it is hard to see exactly what it means or where it leaves us. The civil rights movement, the women's movement, the initiatives toward sexual freedom and responsibility have all taken on a transforming urgency. Many of their ideas have been in the works for more than a century, but since the 1960s we have seen them spread first through our own culture and now around the globe.

We recognize that the human encompasses many colors, many traditions, many wishes, and many ways of seeing. The human potential movements, the liberation movements, the movements for gay and black and indigenous and women's rights not only pose basic questions of who we are as individuals. They also call on us to cultivate a new level of acceptance and mutual respect for our differences.

It is tempting to dismiss all the sloganeering of these movements as so much special pleading. But that would be a serious mistake. For whatever the slogans mean—and though they can and have been very divisive at times—they show how powerfully deep is our new consciousness of the value of the human in and for its diversity, the indispensable Reverence for Life.

The deepest component of this new consciousness is our acknowledgment of the interconnectedness of everything, of the fragility of living systems, their mutual strength and vulnerability. We have a good chance to see that the growing environmental consciousness is very close to spirituality itself, in its inclusiveness, that Schweitzer's stress on Reverence for Life—all life—is part of the new ecological credo. Indeed, among these forces, ecology is in a sense the crown and climax of the others.

The bottom line is that the coming together of these forces is creating the revolution in religion itself. The word *religion* comes from the Latin, *religio, religare*: To connect. To knit together. To include. I take it to mean the energy, the force, the yearning in the human heart and the human brain for inclusiveness, wholeness, togetherness. When this energy flowers, it is extraordinary. When it becomes twisted, it turns to horror. When it becomes irreligious, religion operates as a mode of divisiveness and exclusion, but when it is acting from its real meaning, then it is this marvelous force of continual reformation. It propels people to recognize that each of us is unique and individual.

Spirituality is the name of this force. Spirituality is the presence of what everyone recognizes as the unity of the One and the Many, the All in All. This spirituality is at the core of every religion. When this spirituality is intact and active, religion is alive. When the spirit is missing, so-called religion petrifies, turns into stony fundamentalism, and it kills.

A renewed spirituality, real religion in constant reformation, can transform ourselves and our world.

James Parks Morton   113

Leonard Marks

LEONARD MARKS, a trial lawyer, is a senior partner in the New York law firm of Gold, Farrell and Marks. His clients have included Billy Joel, the Beatles, Madonna, Eddie Murphy, and Michael Jackson. He is media director for the Temple of Understanding.

As a New York trial lawyer and former federal prosecutor, my focus was on advocacy and aggressive argument until I met an Indian Jain, a former monk, who introduced me to meditation. After a few weeks I felt more relaxed, began to come to terms with painful things in my experience, and decided to join—why not?—a small group on a trip to India. Two weeks after arrival, we were taken on a pilgrimage to the holy mountain Palitana.

The night before the three-hour climb, we were instructed to repeat a mantra on each step and concentrate on a core question. Mine was: "How can I release the love I feel trapped inside me?" I repeated mantra and core question on each step. Halfway up the mountain, I had a totally unexpected experience. It was as if light poured into body and mind. Tears poured out. I was stunned. I seemed to see auras of light around plants, animals, people, even rocks, and to hear a whispered: "You are asking the wrong question. Everything that is, is the expression of divine love. Just see; just be."

Life would not be the same again; there was no denying the reality of every sentient being on this planet being awesome—inviolable—from conception to maturation and that the earth itself is the living scripture to be shared by all religions. We all exist through the air we breathe, the water our bodies contain, the earth that feeds us, and the light that awakens us. However different, we are deeply related; we come from the same source; we are interdependent in our creating food, clothing, shelter.

My first criterion of what it means to be human is to protect children, who in this twentieth century have starved to death and have been murdered by the millions. The second priority and criterion is the protection of the planet for future generations. The ancient Iroquois' focus on the seventh generation must be taken seriously and guide our actions. Nuclear weapons and nuclear waste with a deadly half-life of more than twenty thousand years are sheer murderous insanity. The Chernobyl disaster, earthquakes, typhoons, hurricanes may be warnings for us to develop new, non-devastating technologies while there is—perhaps—still time.

My next criterion of humanness is respect for all beings and their religions. We must not allow socially irresponsible governments and religious leaders to provoke war and see "the other" as the enemy, as less than human. Do we really believe in a God who approves the repeated wars that religions have sponsored or encouraged? The United Nations has often ignored and avoided religious issues, but it is more and more important for religious leaders to work with the United Nations on conflict resolution and prevention.

In all nations, religions tell stories of wisdom and hope. In India, there is a story of a highly respected elder who was confronted by youngsters plotting to embarrass him. One youngster held a beautiful bird behind his back. The group said to the elder, "There's a bird; is it alive or dead?" If he replied, "It is alive," the youngster would kill the bird by squeezing its neck to prove the elder was wrong. If he replied, "It is dead," the youngster would release the bird to fly away and again prove the elder wrong. When the youngsters repeated three times, "There's a bird; is it alive or dead?" the elder thought deeply and replied, "It is in your hands."

The criteria of being human are in our hands, and the future of humanity is on our blessed and splendid planet.

Nancy Jack Todd

"Nature and I are two," is Woody Allen's often-quoted pronouncement on his relationship to the natural world. Though we may dismiss it as an exaggerated—and misinformed claim by a New Yorker, most of us understand what he means. And it is still the way the culture at large, nationally and globally, behaves with stagger-

NANCY JACK TODD is an environmental writer and editor. A cofounder of ecological design think tanks, the New Alchemy Institute and Ocean Arks International, she currently publishes the periodical *Annals of Earth*.

ing and increasing momentum. And I am forced to admit that there are times, when faced, for example, with determined guerrilla raids on my garden by marauding woodchucks, or the sight of a tick burrowing into a child's soft skin, I lapse into dualism akin to that of Woody Allen's. Forgetting momentarily that all life is structured by the same DNA code, and shares in the ongoing exchange of air, water, and nutrients, I clearly view nature and I as two and adamantly opposed.

Ironically, it is through my garden that I am most readily restored to my more usual sense of the human–natural continuum. Growing organic vegetables, herbs, berries, and cutting flowers for my family and friends—nourishment for the body and the soul—stirs in me a satisfaction bordering on solemn contentment. And it is often in my woods-bordered garden that I have had encounters with wild creatures other than woodchucks that have been a source of profound delight to me.

One damp June day, kneeling on the ground to seed lettuce, I thought I spotted a new kind of beetle. The beetle appeared to be gold, the gold of tawny honey. I paused to watch where it was going. It remained immobile for several minutes and then suddenly hopped toward me. At closer range I discovered my beetle to be a frog, a minute and exquisite creature, the size of a fingernail. When it hesitated in its flight I could see the delicate details of its perfect and intelligent feet and a light stripe over its amber eyes. I froze, transfixed, for as long as it chose to favor me with its presence. My frog stayed for a few minutes before it hopped off again to disappear under the sheltering leaves of a hollyhock. I walk, since then, with heightened mindfulness lest I disrupt the daily perambulations of small golden frogs who might still find my garden their sort of place.

The countless mysteries of the nonhuman world have long proved an inexhaustible source of both investigation and inspiration to scientists and artists as well as gardeners and naturalists.

The concerned environmentalist E. O. Wilson, through his research on the subject of biophilia, has thought long and deeply about our relationship to our home planet and what, if any, aspects of it we can draw upon in an attempt not to destroy the source of our being. In the summer of 1992 he convened a conference to discuss what he has called the biophilia hypothesis. In essence, *biophilia* means love of or affinity for life.

The question with which Dr. Wilson and his colleagues were grappling was whether there is credible evidence for our having inherited a genetically coded bond with life other than human. In his own words, "Biophilia, if it exists, and I believe that it exists, is the innately emotional affiliation of human beings to other living organisms. Innate means hereditary and hence part of ultimate human nature."

That there is evidence that we are not, as a species, irrevocably alienated from the natural world gives us a solid rationale to continue the struggle toward more sustainable societies. Science in the form of the biophilia hypothesis suggests that we have reasonable grounds to believe we are capable of an affirmation of life as an essential part of what makes us what we are. This being so, the healing energy working its way through so many disparate and multiple channels may yet coalesce into a dynamic strong enough to counter the destructive forces that otherwise seem so overwhelming. Dr. Schweitzer urges: "We must strive together to attain to a theory of the universe affirmative of the world and of life." More and more people are so striving—and increasingly together.

Patrick Clarke

PATRICK CLARKE is a Brazilian priest and educator who was an assistant to the late Paulo Freire working in literacy and adult education.

Sometimes a gift can change your life, transform you so that you are never the same again. It happened to me one Christmas Eve. I was trudging home downcast through the narrow dark alleys of a shantytown. It was raining and I was lonely. I wanted to be with my own people. Just this once. To share the warmth and intimacy of Christmas in familiar surroundings. To recall childhood and youth. To return to that hearth which had nurtured me, and which I had left behind so many years before.

Suddenly, a voice pierced the rainy darkness, interrupting my nostalgic reverie. I stopped, looked about, but saw no one. As I moved away, I heard my name called again. This time, as I turned, Francisca, a woman of the night, emerged from the shadows, arms open to embrace me, to perform the ritual that she had enacted every time we had met through all the years we had known each other.

It was, as always, the briefest of encounters. She hugged me, stroked my face, held my hands, asked me about my health, my family, my life. Her interest was sincere, intense, utterly transparent. A ministry of healing, of consolation. "Francisca," I said as we were about to part, "remember to pray for me, please."

She stepped back, fixed me with an eye that was half-compassion, half-reproach, and said, "Child, don't you know, by now, that you live in my heart?"

And so saying, she disappeared, through the cracks in the darkness, back into the night's trade, as I sprouted wings of hope, joy, gratitude for the coming of this Christ figure that gifted my darkness and whom I will carry in my heart for all my days.

The spiritual malaise of our time is an epidemic that is destroying the fabric of our Western psyche. It is the loss of innocence and wonder, the death of adventure, and the conversion of the "gift" into a commodity. It is a culture where everything is negotiable, in which, to reverse the memorable words of Chief Seattle, "We do not belong to the earth; the earth belongs to us." This has had and is having catastrophic consequences for the interrelationship of all living things, because the predatory and aggressive nature of human intervention is based not on reverence for the gift that all life is but on the satisfaction of immediate and individualistic consumer fantasies, which, on ultimate analysis, are destructively addictive.

There is no way out of this bare room except through the process of *re-ligare*, which immediately removes it from the realm of mere humanism, for the humanist utopia by itself is incapable of generating the imaginative spiritual energy required to reverse the tide of neobarbarism. In my view, we must reencounter the mystical/contemplative tradition still very much alive in many cultures that have not yet been "civilized/humanized" and are still surprisingly robust in places like Ireland, with its long history of mythical and mystical adventuring.

Without that tradition to sustain the human project the spirit of the "gift" will be destroyed, and the structure and cohesion of faithfulness and gratitude (which are the very essence of our being and becoming) will degenerate to the stage where people are neither friends nor real aliens but cordial strangers, sustained by creditor–debtor relationships in the context of the jostle of the market—which is not the hustle of life.

Life is possible only in that social context in which the gift, once received, can be passed on by the receiver. It is a society in which a person's and a people's grandeur (as a young Macuxi Indian in Roraima, Brazil, once said to me) consists in "having nothing," that is, in being able to receive the gift, then pass it on. History is replete with barbarous devastation by greed, power, and intolerance. Yet everywhere communities do exist in the midst of barbaric chaos, communities that believe that all life is a "gift," to be savored, lived, and passed on. In that way, its returns are an undreamt-of abundance: Francisca's open arms of our humanness.

Arno Gruen

To have a human identity is to know pain, to acknowledge helplessness, and to be capable of compassion. If we come to fear pain, helplessness, compassion as denoting weakness, we become inhuman. Inhumanity stands in direct relation to the failure to develop an identity of one's own.

ARNO GRUEN is a psychologist and psychology professor in Zurich, Switzerland. He is the author of several books, including *The Betrayal of the Self* and *The Loss of Compassion and the Politics of Indifference*.

If we are not loved as children for what we are but rather for fulfilling the expectations of others, we cannot develop an identity of our own. Failing to develop such an identity, we lay the foundation for our inhumanity.

In the title of his devastating yet lovingly written report on Auschwitz, *If This Is a Man*, Primo Levi questions by implication what it means to be a human being, thus pointing far beyond the phenomenon of Auschwitz alone.

Auschwitz is neither the beginning nor the end of the shame we must feel over what human beings are capable of. This shame began with the infanticide of antiquity and continues today with the daily mutilation and rape of women and children, of human beings, in South America, Africa, and former Yugoslavia, Russia, the Near East, and here in Europe with the violent acts prompted by hatred of foreigners as well as those committed by children against other children. We proudly call the world a "civilized" one, and yet our laws and technologies have developed a life of their own that is hostile toward our psychological and physical survival. "The political situation vacillates between consolidation of bureaucratic power and outbreaks of impotent rage." (E. R.Wolfe)

We live in a world in which we are more and more dependent on one another, and yet it is also a world in which we are turning increasingly against one another. Why is this so? Why is Reverence for Life so rarely experienced and contempt for life so endemic?

Everyone has experienced helplessness and powerlessness. The helplessness of childhood is no doubt the most formative experience for every human being, far more so than for other species of animals. If a baby chimpanzee is injured, it is immediately picked up and cared for by its mother; in the case of humans, it is not unusual for the mother or father to become angry and to punish rather than help the child. Recently, at a skating rink, a little girl fell down and hurt her face. Her parents were furious and punished her by making her go home. The psychological wounds that children experience every day provide the basis for a profound distortion in human development that determines our whole being, our very identity. We are taught from early childhood on that we must not admit we have been hurt because that is an admission of helplessness. Our vulnerability thus comes to denote being at the mercy of someone else. This makes helplessness an unbearable condition that robs us of self-esteem.

And so our civilization breeds the all-pervasive need of being as invulnerable as possible. We strive for possessions, power and status in order to feel secure, to save ourselves from the intolerable awareness of a self experienced as weak and insignificant.

It is a terrible paradox that the very disintegration of authoritarian structures, a process that could foster freedom, creativity, and spontaneity, leads almost without exception to a counteraction. People feel threatened by insecurity and uncertainty. They believe they are struggling for freedom and security by struggling for a "higher" form of identity—namely, one based on ethnic and linguistic homogeneity. Xenophobia and nationalism are desperate attempts to compensate for an impaired feeling of self-esteem and of inner emptiness by means of symbolism and symbolic actions instead of facing their emptiness and its causes.

These causes lie in a form of child raising in which children are taught to value themselves not for their own aliveness but for adapting to behavior patterns characterized by fear of vulnerability and fear of compassion. This is where the feeling of emptiness originates.

As early as 1932 Sandor Ferenczi wrote that abused children "feel physically and morally helpless; their personality is not sufficiently consolidated for them to be able to protest even in their thoughts. Their fear, when it reaches a peak of intensity, automatically forces them to submit to the will of the aggressor, to intuit and obey his every wish, to forget themselves entirely, to identify totally with the aggressor."

This identification with the aggressor has dire political consequences. It leads to a devastating social behavior pattern, to an alliance between victim and victimizer, and simultaneously to the victim's hatred of those who can be called weak. The latter become the enemy because they symbolize the victim within ourselves, the alive person we could have become but who was destroyed because we learned to fear that such aliveness would threaten our connection to our parents. This is why people search for enemies, for without them an individual cannot sustain a personality structure based on self-rejection and self-hatred.

If we identify with the aggressor, we lose access to our own feelings. *Stolen Childhood* presents the story of children who have become emotionally impoverished. They are unable to cry or to rejoice, for their awareness of their vulnerability has been taken from them. In this vein, a member of the National Guard under the Nicaraguan dictator Somoza said in an interview: "I'm small and skinny. Before I joined the National Guard, I was afraid of everything and everyone . . . [Today] I'm not afraid anymore. That is the most important thing. . . . That's what I call being a man." For men like this, cruelty, violence, and contempt for pain and suffering are the necessary components of their behavior. Their own need for love and succor is experienced as weakness, and therefore being violent gives them a feeling of strength. This is why xenophobes and right-wing extremists are obsessed by the idea that they must exterminate foreigners (whether Jews, Italians, Mexicans, or Blacks), the weak, and the disabled.

It was not our distant ancestors who tried to escape their pain. It is we who—lacking a true self, lacking a real identity—cling to the delusion that we can be saved by a "strength" that is to be achieved by means of racial and ethnic hatred.

Someone who grows up without real love cannot become an authentic human being. For this reason a clergyman in Hoyerswerda, the German town where radical right-wing youth first attacked foreigners, regarded the violent acts they committed to be "consequences of the absence of love in the lives of the children of this community." That is why the hatred felt by the unloved is a threat to us all.

What are we to do? Everywhere, those who are filled with hatred do not know who it is they really hate. Therefore, hatred must first be accepted as something justifiable—to the extent that it stems from the aggressive rage that was a reaction to the original aggressors. It must then be redirectd to the forgotten, repressed, split-off objects that caused it. The goal must be to recognize the hatred as having been diverted from the real objects—inadequate parents, teachers, schools, etc.—not to repress it. But there is a precondition for reaching this goal.

We must oppose violence unhesitatingly and authoritatively. We must take decisive action against those who attack women and children, the defenseless, and the weak with incendiary bombs, artillery barrages, and poison gas. Only this will stop the perpetrators. When, however, politicians underestimate the role of hatred or even legitimize it, then democracy is endangered. It is not true that this hatred can be mitigated by allowing it to be expressed, in the sense of "letting off steam." The trouble is that hatred which denies its true origins begins to develop a life of its own. Therefore, every individual destructive act intensifies the rage of such people. They are able to suppress their guilt feelings only through more destructiveness. This is another reason why the stereotypical thinking of politicians, which minimizes the danger of hatred, actually fosters destructiveness.

Dealing firmly and consistently with the perpetrators of violence "liberates" them from the need to intensify their violence. Thus, since 1991, violent right-wing extremism has been reduced in the German state of Saxony, where the government has taken a firm position but at the same time has also dealt with the emotional problems involved. Failure to take an unequivocal stance against violence and to respond to it with firmness is equivalent to supporting the perpetrators in denying their guilt; we prevent them from confronting their own feelings of guilt. When we do this, we are digging our own graves, for if we make it impossible for the violent to rediscover the human potential still within them, we become their victims. If we learn to understand the political ramifications of the process of identifying with the aggressor and recognize this tendency in ourselves, it will lead to the consistently firm approach we need to bring about solutions. Then we will stop looking for victims instead of for those who are really responsible for our malaise. We must learn to recognize the violent among us as caught up in a vicious cycle of submissive obedience and the hatred to which that gives rise. We must learn to see what we are doing to one another, how we employ Schweitzer's ethic and Reverence for Life in practice.

It is not political ideologies that will lead us out of our present impasse but rather our persistent efforts to be honest with ourselves.

(*Translated by Hildegarde and Hunter Hannum*)

Robert Aitken

To be human is to practice being human, as distinguished from being an alligator. It is to acknowledge and transmute alligator energy into human work. It is to protect alligators, the real ones and the metaphorical ones, who are also real.

ROBERT AITKEN, ROSHI, is a retired master of the Honolulu Diamond Sangha, a Zen Buddhist Society. He lives in Puna, on the Big Island of Hawaii.

TO BE HUMAN IS TO LEARN WHAT IT IS TO BE HUMAN AND THEN TO PRACTICE IT. It is to stand fast in the face of inhumanity, whatever the cost. It is to stand fast and to conspire with others in their human practice.

TO BE HUMAN IS TO TAKE JOY IN MEANING. It is to realize harmony, affinity, and commonality and to express that realization. It is to respect the dynamics of relationships and to clarify them. It is to delight in the unique nature of each individual person, family, culture, region, bush, stone, cat, mongoose, and duck—and to express that delight. It is to honor and revere the unknown, to revere life in its plurality of oneness, its oneness in plurality.

Anne E. Goldfeld

ANNE E. GOLDFELD is an infectious disease specialist and assistant professor at the Harvard Medical School. She has worked as a doctor in Cambodia and Africa and has written numerous articles on human rights, refugees, and land-mine catastrophes.

In October of 1994, I worked as a general doctor in Zaire at the Mugunga Refugee Camp, which at the time housed approximately 150,000 Rwandan refugees, near Goma.

I came to work with the American Refugee Committee to help set up a health center in this expanse of human squalor and suffering, where I was reminded once again of the essence of what it means to be human as well as the consequences of the breakdown of human connection.

In the spring and summer of 1994, over 1 million people died in Rwanda. The world sat mesmerized and impotent in front of television reports—showing rivers of hacked, murdered Tutsi bodies—as we asked ourselves, What should be our human response?

The United Nations, whose birth was to prevent just such a genocide, had failed miserably. And as July drew to a close, some 2 million Hutus fled across the border into Zaire in less than two weeks. Once the Hutus were in Goma, mass death continued; the assassin was cholera. Among the refugees were both the Hutu perpetrators of the genocide and an estimated twenty thousand orphans; as in most refugee situations, the vast majority of the camp's population was women and children.

Mugunga had grown up literally overnight on hostile volcanic rock, at the base of the Virunga rain forest. I arrived in Goma on Saturday. On Sunday we finished putting up the center's tents. And on Monday at 9:00 A.M. when we opened the Mugunga center, masses of people had gathered pushing at the ropes. There were dead bodies wrapped in mats and people lying half-dead from malaria or diarrhea or pneumonia or starvation. The first day we saw over 500 patients.

In one of its first days of operation, a young man wrapped in a blanket was brought to the health center. His neighbors found him—he was alone in the camp—with severe diarrhea. He had gotten so weak that he could not stand up and go to the latrine, so he just lay in his feces in his blanket until he was brought to us. As we pulled away the blanket, flies flew out at us; liquid stool covered his body, and the stench was almost unbearable. When his clothes were cut away, an emaciated body of perhaps sixty pounds emerged. As we washed him, his naked shrunken, lethargic body glistened in the bright volcanic sunlight.

He was familiar—he had been among the walking corpses that Eisenhower's troops found when they entered Buchenwald, and he was a starving newly widowed Cambodian peasant woman. His face had flashed across the news reports as he was brutalized in the carnage of Bosnia. Here in Mugunga, he was a nameless dying boy victimized by war and a barbarism that once again was not prevented by a world and a humanity that had looked away until it was too late.

Despite the United Nations claims that there were adequate supplies in the camp, everywhere in Mugunga there were mothers with shriveled dry breasts and skinny babies with barely the strength to cry, all set in relief by the well-fed Hutu soldiers patrolling the camp. There was the grandmother who brought in her fifteen-month-old grandson who was coughing. His mother was very sick and now he was, too. She said that this listless, sunken-eyed, emaciated child had been a big boy. A sore was beginning to form on the hanging skin covering his protruding hipbone where all his muscle seemed to have dissolved away.

In the aftermath of the exodus of over 2 million refugees from Rwanda to Zaire in the summer of 1994, the United Nations claimed it was forced to quickly set up distribution lines for food and plastic sheeting for shelter. They distributed these through the political structures in the camp, which meant that the food and sheeting were first tithed to the Hutu military, and the estimated 30 percent of women heads of households were out of luck. And so in October we were literally seeing women and children—many homeless—starving to death despite the fact that 170 metric tons of food were entering the camp on a daily basis.

When a young man fell off a truck on the main road into Goma the gravel ripped the skin off half of his face and he sustained a bad tear near his left eye and mouth—it was clear that he would greatly benefit from a skillful surgeon. Among the newly arrived German medical team was a young gynecological surgeon named Otto. It was Otto's first day in Mugunga, or in any refugee camp for that matter, and he was overwhelmed. As I told him of the boy, he looked at me with extreme apprehension and said he needed his nurse. As Otto began to work on the boy, with our less than ideal sutures and lighting, he said he needed a better sterile field. The nurse who ran the wound tent gently said, "Look, Otto, there are flies all over; I don't think we are going to do better on a sterile field." Otto's nurse couldn't speak English. After struggling for a while with the communication, I gave up and asked her in Yiddish if she would mind if I spoke to her in Yiddish—it was so close to German I was sure she would understand me. She nodded yes as though it were a perfectly common occurrence for someone to ask her that question. Yiddish, German, and English intertwined and floated upward like divine sparks as we worked. And so, in the wound tent of the health center at Mugunga, fifty years after the Holocaust, the daughters and sons of that terrible war worked to save the face of a Rwandan boy who had survived another genocide. I felt hopeful for the next generation of Hutus and Tutsis.

In the Talmud a discussion between the great rabbinic sages Meir and Eliezer is recounted. Rabbi Eliezer asks Rabbi Meir, "Where can I find the messiah?" "You can find him at the 'Dung Gate' of the walled city of Jerusalem," Rabbi Meir answers.

"At the Dung Gate, where the lepers are outcast?" questions a dubious Rabbi Eliezer. "And how will I recognize him?"

"You will know him," says Rabbi Meir. "He sits among the lepers near the gate, where he bandages their sores one by one."

At the end of one of my last days in Mugunga, a young, very gaunt widow approached me with a malnourished three-year-old. We bought her a bowl of beans and potatoes, only to discover moments later a young starving, emaciated orphan girl of perhaps ten years. But we were out of money. Extremely discouraged, we began to search for a way to get more food when, turning back, I saw that the young widow had invited the girl to share her food— the baby, the stranger girl, and the young mother were all scooping up potatoes and beans from a shared bowl with their hands. What would I have done if I were in the young mother's place?

And it is with awe that one recognizes that one is on holy ground where a starving survivor of a genocide again teaches what it means to be human, where if one does not look away, one comes face-to-face with the Buddha-nature, with the spirit of the one who said, *"Inasmuch as you did it to the least of my sisters and brothers . . . ,"* where one is comforted by *El Mole Rachamin,* our God who is full of compassion and who suffers with us.

James Finn Cotter

JAMES FINN COTTER, a professor of English at Mount Saint Mary College, Newburgh, New York, has written on Dante, Chaucer, Sidney, and Hopkins. He is president of the International Hopkins Association and a translator of *The Divine Comedy*.

To be fully human is to be full of God. Not full of myself, because I am as deep as a saucer and as trustworthy as a snake. "We have met the enemy and he is us," according to Pogo. I would change that insight to read, less grammatically but more accurately, "I have met the enemy and he is me." Not because I am neurotic or guilt-ridden but because I have reason so often to be disappointed and shocked at my own behavior toward others, in words that brush off or cut down and harm, with actions that injure or betray, and by thoughts that mock, molest, or even murder. To find the evil polluting this century, I do not have to look far. The barbaric inhuman, *c'est moi.*

What is it to be human? I see the sun rise behind the dark blue ridge of Mount Beacon and shine into my bedroom window to awake me from sleep. The gift of another day is mine to be lived in loving intimacy with God and those I meet today and recall from yesterday and long ago. God greets the day and them in me, and me, with each other and with all, I begin again without ending in awe for life's hallowed Mystery.

To be human is to let God be human in us.

Gillian Kean

I accept one Supreme Reality
Of which all creation is the
    echo,
I renounce any attempt to
    judge
What is, from what is not,
    Divine.
I intend to recognize the
    Absolute
In every aspect of experience
    which impinges on me.

GILLIAN KEAN has been involved in peace and peace education since her childhood in England during World War II. She currently works with the Dandelion Trust, devoted to the continuation and healing of this world among worlds.

I see all parts of the Whole without prejudice.
I recognize the seen as a pale shadow of the Unseen.
And all this separation as Unity.
And I trust in all, through All
That there is no darkness forever and ever in this
moment,
Which eternally oscillates with That which is,
An ever-moving stillness.
I welcome the Peace that is present

In every second without exception,
Even when it appears to be a turmoil,
Trusting that in every disturbance is a Peace.
I accept my wholeness
By accepting myself as I am.
I accept my wholeness
By offering myself as I am.
I accept my wholeness
as Holy through all apparent faults.
I recognize Love as the only Reality
and in Love all peace and plenty.
I renounce all opinion and accept the Whole.
I own the selfishness of my small self
As a sign that I am more than I think I am.
I welcome the dark as the light's shadow.
I accept all that I am without
To realize all that I am within.
And I dedicate all I seem to be
To all that I Really am,
In gratitude and wonder
So that All may
Glory Be.

Catharina Halkes

CATHARINA HALKES is an emeritus professor of theology at the University of Nymegen in the Netherlands. She is a feminist theologian who held the first European professorship in feminism and Christianity.

Being human implies being humane, but both are far from synonymous, for being human may mean no more than being genetically part of our species wherever it lives on earth. Being humane, I feel, denotes something positive, a value about the best that we humans can give to one another. It includes relatedness, bonding, solidarity, love, succor where it is needed. It implies responsibility for one another and doing justice to one another. For we are ambiguous creatures, as is so clearly expressed in the common usage that judges dubious conduct as being "all too human" or some attitudes and misconduct as being "barely human." There is no greater compliment than, "You are so human." We humans are all too subject to the downward pull of the gravity of our appetites and passions. And yet at the same time we are pulled upward against all that gravity by an inner call, an ideal, a vocation well beyond our limits. This tension has through the ages been the inspiration of the poet, the storyteller, the dramatist, the artist. In the course of time this pull in two directions has resulted in much that is positive and life-enhancing and in much that is extremely negative. I am inclined to think that these rhythms of forever falling, forever rising must be inherent to our human specificity and determine our conduct as long as it remains prereflective. Only from the moment we allow awareness to arise, this pull to transcending ego, this overcoming of our inborn egocentricity, may begin to guide, become a lodestar on our way to full consciousness of the Mystery of life in which we participate.

During these waning decades of our century there has been a strong tendency in Western culture to "pull ourselves together." It became an ideal, even a compulsion, to be maximally "self-supporting," even "self-asserting," to "stand up for oneself." The entire emphasis was on playing as forceful a role in the power game of the "free" market as possible, using the most sophisticated technologies, all leading to an ever more intensified egocentricity. The economy, high tech, money, nationalistic hubris became the omnipotent idols subverting our culture, destroying human relationships, estranging us from all "human," in the sense of humane, feelings for one another and for nature itself.

Instead of seeing our lives as the inner human process unfolding, as participation and reciprocity, in striving for a higher quality of being, we resignedly submit to the idolatrous antivalues of "having," of profit, of conquest and domination, whatever the cost to "the others," to "them," all of nature included. The total eclipse of norms and values has led to the total eclipse of our humanness. The "liberal" idea of freedom, perverted into the denial of the limits of that freedom by discounting responsibility, resulted in a hegemony of egocentricity that could not have happened without the spectacular dereliction of the religions, of which the influence on human conduct had become minimal.

The Enlightenment had—apart from its often fully justified critique, its questionings, and its unmasking of spiritual tyrannies—

undermined the West's spiritual roots. Churches, belief systems, religions had revealed themselves as ambivalent forces, on the one hand inspirational but on the other hand all too infantilizing and regressive in their static dogmatism, traditionalism, their habits of coercion, their lust for institutional power, but, perhaps above all, their frozen feudal God image, caricature of a plausible living God.

I am deeply convinced that one of the causes of our social and human deterioration may be ascribed to the masculinization of both humans and God. Aeons of reverence for the feminine principle, for nature and fertility, were succeeded by a patriarchal system in which all the stress was on the passivity of nature and on the linear principle of a culture dominated by the masculine principle. Humankind became mankind; the human being became Man; God became a Father with all the male attributes of fighter, warrior, ruler, and despot. There is truth in Mary Daly's dictum: "If God is male, the male is God." Myth and image may clarify correlations among the phenomena of existence, as religion and poetry prove beyond doubt. Religion, however, is always at risk of distorting the imagery, of subverting it into norms and laws imposed to be obeyed on penalty of eternal damnation. It no longer inspires but chains people to distorted modes of consciousness, however obsolete.

The religions have indeed the potential of opening the way to higher levels of consciousness, but all too often and all too obviously they prove to be hurdles on the way. This is our situation so that at the moment we find ourselves in a vacuum of spiritual emptiness and lack of direction. My hope and concern is that this is a temporary state of affairs and that this vacuum will be pierced in the search for new beginnings which may lead to a turnabout toward life-affirming, creative attitudes, away from the hegemony of the masculine principle, and that the feminine principle will be restored, the source of all life will once again be unblocked, polarization overcome, and the diversity of forms and aspects of reality be evaluated as being enriching and the reciprocity and relatedness among all beings realized.

Although humankind consists of two genders, nevertheless for millennia it was dominated by one of these. The dominant males with their priorities of analysis, competition, abstraction, and power, wreaked endless injustice on women, held them in contempt as strangers and paupers, sold them as slaves and chattel. The feminine principle is not absent in men but is of course stronger in women. Women experience it in the cyclic rhythms of their bodies; that keeps them closer to the rhythms of nature, more respectful toward the earth. The ancient creation myths of Genesis, replete with profound stories and imagery, demand new readings, a new openness to their meanings for our time, for they are to be reinterpreted in ever-changing contexts. They are not enumerations of historical facts but stories that reflect the ongoing process of unfolding, of Matter, of Life, of Spirit, of Person, in which each and all are participants. I see the sustaining power in the Divine Spirit, at once transcendent and immanent, that animates all of Creation and each one of us. I see in Jesus of Nazareth the human being who opens himself to this Mystery until he becomes a "transparent" manifestation of the Divine, an exemplar on the life journey of each one of us. For the Divine Principle, the Spirit was breathed into each one of us. Not only we must change, but also our unjust structures must change, for the delusions and idols that dominate our time cannot be defeated except by our solidarity. Could we not form small groupings, countless cells of humans, mutually bonded, to resist and overcome the evil powers of our time, persist in "living them away" in a commitment to the world that is indispensable—a commitment to Reverence for Life?

(*Translated by Frederick Franck*)

Catharina Halkes   141

Dean Frantz

DEAN FRANTZ is a Jungian analyst in Fort Wayne, Indiana. He is the author of a monograph, *The Seasons of Life*.

As I grow older, and especially after being diagnosed with a life-threatening illness, I have given considerable thought to my own death and its ramifications for daily life.

The link with the infinite, the detachment of which Meister Eckhart spoke, implies that my life cannot be ruled by the daily news headlines. It suggests that I dare not dwell on the petty little problems which consume precious energy. It assures me that although I am a citizen of this world, I also have citizenship in the cosmos. Detachment reminds me that life is to be lived consciously and that every moment is to be treasured. It also changes my view of reality. It is so easy to be caught up in the illusion that the real can be measured, weighed, counted, valued in dollars, or tested by the five senses.

Jung commented on this when he wrote about two dreams, one in 1944 after the illness which almost claimed his life and the other three years before his death: "The aim of both these dreams is to effect a reversal of the relationship between ego-consciousness and the unconscious as the generator of the empirical personality," he said. "This reversal suggests that in the opinion of the 'other side' our unconscious existence is the real one and our conscious world is a kind of illusion."

This makes it possible for us to contact the infinite within our finite container and also encourages that detachment which opens the door to whatever lies beyond death.

Cornel West

CORNEL WEST, an author, philosopher, critic, and activist, is professor of Afro-American studies and professor in the divinity school at Harvard University. He has written twelve books, including the best-seller *Race Matters*. Cornel West's contribution is from a convocation address of the 197th Year of Harvard Divinity School as printed in the 1995 *Harvard Divinity School Bulletin*.

What are we to do with the problem of evil? How do we come to terms with undeserved harm, unjustified suffering, and unmerited pain? If there is no overarching philosophical way of resolving the problem, how do we deal with the existential scars and wounds and bruises that affect each and every one of us, but that disproportionately affect the least of these?

To come to terms with the problem of evil in my own way I had to come to terms, of course, with white supremacy, a thoroughly modern construct of race, first put forward by François Bernier in 1684, canonized by Linnaeus in 1734 in his *Natural System* and in Buffon's *Natural History* in 1735. It became a science by the nineteenth century. The discourse and practice of positively charged whiteness and negatively debased blackness and brownness and redness and yellowness would fundamentally shape what we understand modernity to be. I look forward to dialogue with my sophisticated and distinguished colleagues who are preoccupied with modernity but who have yet to meet the challenge of the fundamental role of white supremacy and its European imperial and colonial manifestations in the modern period. It is not that they are wrong. They just need a little broadening and deepening. For what? For their quest for truth and knowledge in highbrow scholarly inquiry that is part and parcel of our own self-understanding and of being part of this highly privileged community.

White supremacy generates a profound sense of the absurd, especially among people of African descent, since they are targeted. We were reminded of this only recently on the floor of the United States Senate. After six decades we witnessed the abandonment of a national obligation to dependent children primarily because it has a black face on it. Senator Edward Kennedy is right; we are going to look back on what happened as a turning point. White supremacy in its subtle forms still goes on, and we don't need brother Mark Fuhrman to remind us of the more explicit forms. We still have to deal with that sense of the absurd—that we view something so irrational and capricious and arbitrary as skin pigmentation as a benchmark of one's humanity, as the mark of whether one is inside or outside or on the margins of the human family.

We are all featherless, two-legged, linguistically conscious creatures born between urine and feces. Saint Jerome and Sigmund Freud and Bill Clinton have all reminded us that we all emerge in the funk. I can put on my three-piece suit if I want to, but I emerged among the juices and the fluids and the stink and the stench as a little baby hollering out for help and protection, hoping for a little love and care and meaning as I meet inevitable and inescapable and unavoidable extinction someday very soon.

We are not here long. What are we going to do in that short time as we encounter the absurd, as we encounter the various insults and attacks on one's beauty? A whole culture in the past (and still, partly, in the present) was organized to convince black folk they have the wrong hips and lips and noses and hair texture and skin pigmentation. That is visceral. That is bodily—being in a debased black body, dealing with beauty and ugliness as a way of providing some source of self-confidence and self-affirmation, especially in a market-driven, image-centered culture. What kinds of scars are left? Or what about the scars against black intelligence? The Bell Curve, of course, is but one manifestation among a whole host of others. It is a way of raising the question that is already a subtle attack.

But we are reminded in that wonderful sense of the comic that one often finds among all oppressed people, be they Irish, or Jews, or Armenians, or black folk. Leading European intellectuals concluded in the eighteenth century that no black person had any intelligence whatsoever. In the nineteenth century, most concluded that a few black people had some intelligence. Now we are told that all black people are less than average. We are making progress according to white supremacist criteria. But the very framework is absurd. It is so tendentious, so biased. It becomes a legitimate scholarly inquiry just to ask why "these folk"—after 244 years of chattel and inheritable slavery, when it was against the law to learn how to read, after eighty-one years of Jim and Jane Crow, after fifty-one years when every two and a half days some black child or black man or black woman was hanging from some tree—don't take tests the same way we do.

There is nothing wrong with taking tests, nothing wrong with the dialogue. I am a thoroughgoing libertarian when it comes to putting forward sense and nonsense. Let it flow. Let the critical dialogue take place. But I am talking about a broader sense of history that proceeds from my own particular Christian focus. It has to do with the blood of that cross on Calvary, blood that is inseparable from blood that flows this very moment in prisons, in workplaces, and in high places.

If I were the last person alive in a world that was thoroughly dominated by tribal forces and fueled by parochial hatreds and market forces that are preoccupied with efficiency and productivity but that play down inequality and isolation, I would still hold onto that dialectic of particularism and universalism. That would allow me, at my best, not to lose sight of the humanity of each and every one of us. That is what has, in part, sustained my own sanity as I have tried to come to terms with the problem of evil.

It takes tremendous audacity and a deep sense of folly, the same folly Erasmus wrote about in 1511, to be a Christian at the end of this dreadful and ghastly century. Think about it. Two hundred million fellow human beings murdered in the name of some pernicious ideology. Nazism in the heart of Europe. Stalinism in Russia. Imperialism. Colonialism. Vicious atrocities. In America, patriarchal households and the workers movement that was not allowed to organize collectively until the 1930s, after the system had already nearly collapsed. Jim Crow, Jane Crow. What a century!

My message is that we hold on, to the deep, tragic, comic sense of history that implicates each and every one of us but that also empowers each and every one of us to expound the scope of our empathy and compassion—what Christians call love. Love in all of its fullness means being able to say to the other: "What are you going through? Can I be of service? I won't save you. You won't save me. We won't save America. We won't save the world. But maybe we could make it just a little bit better."

Maybe we can organize. Maybe we can mobilize. Maybe we can sustain a living vision so that the tradition of struggle for decency and dignity remains viable and vibrant, so that the struggle for democracy remains alive and not simply part of a rhetorical deployment to conceal the oligarchic character of our economy.

We must be honest enough with ourselves to say that even without that kind of rational certainty we have a spiritual confidence to stay sane and to sustain ourselves, owing to nonmarket values like love and care, concern and kindness and sweetness.

Joan Chittister

To ask what it means to be human strikes at the fabric of the soul. The temptation, of course, is to gloss, to idealize. The task, however, requires much more than that. The task is not to rhapsodize; it is to distinguish between the human and the nonhuman, the subhuman that rages under it, taxing our humanity at every turn. Then, the task becomes plain. In Thomas Hardy's words, "If way to the better there be, we must look first at the worst."

JOAN CHITTISTER, OSB, is executive director of Bentivision, a research and resource center for contemporary spirituality. She is an international lecturer and widely published author.

The problem with trying to define what it means to be human is that we now take so much of the inhuman for granted. We confuse the meaning of the words *natural* and *human*, make synonyms of them. We act as if one is the other. We allow one to be the other. We rip to shreds the ideas, each of them masks, forgetting one and surrendering to the other. We call the "natural" human and in one flash of the pen presume we have made it so. We wander in a philosophical maze and never even realize that we are lost.

War is "natural," they tell us. Violence is "natural," they argue. Self-aggrandizement is "natural," they maintain. What they do not say is that just because something is "natural" does not make it human. And then the slippage starts, the desecration of life. Greed is "only human," they maintain. Sexism is the will of God, they insist. Rape becomes a weapon of war, of "defense," of the humiliation of one male by another at the expense of women. In a mind-set such as that, ambition is not only condoned; it is encouraged. Dishonesty becomes the coin of the land. Bankers cheat, brokers steal, presidents lie, and the rest of us lower our standards to meet the norm and concentrate more on survival than we do on life. We begin to pay more attention to what we are getting out of life than what we are putting into it.

We still cluck at rape, of course, shake our heads about genocide, and talk about being bored with TV murder trials; we cease to look at the pictures of long-lost children, memorialized on milk cartons. We buy more locks and more guns and insurance policies, hire more lawyers. But we change nothing in ourselves or in anything else. We simply become more and more inured to the "natural" and less and less confident that humanity is a star to be followed or anything more than a brass ring on a boardwalk carousel where fantasy reigns and the process of going someplace is to trace an interminable circle. Humanity goes in and out of focus, blurred always by the "natural" and unconscious of the spiritual that magnetizes it.

But I have seen humanity. I know its face even when I cannot define it. It is blazoned in my mind. It measures my character and condemns my disregard. Anything less than these images disappoints me to the core.

I have a picture in my mind of nuns putting flowers in the gun barrels of Filipino soldiers in Manila who then refused to shoot into the crowd. I still hold in my heart the sight of a young man in Tiananmen Square standing in front of a moving tank that then turned back. I carry the image of men carrying a lone survivor out of a tangle of earthquake wreckage on a swaying overpass that then collapsed. Every time these images flash before my mind I remember that to be human is to give yourself for things far greater than yourself.

I have a memory, too, as a twelve-year-old crying silently, bitterly, facedown into a pillow on the living room floor. That day, my bird, my only life companion, had disappeared up an open flue in our apartment wall. There were visiting relatives in the house, in my bedroom, whom I knew were not to be disturbed. The needs of the guest came first, I had been taught. But when the house was safely dark, I let the pain pour out, not simply for the loss of my dearest possession but also in sorrow for my own carelessness in his regard. Then, suddenly, I felt the covers around me tighten. My mother had gotten in on one side of the mattress, my father on the other, and together they held me all the long and empty night. I learned then that being human meant to enter into someone else's pain.

I heard a young U.S. soldier talk enthusiastically about gunning down Iraqi soldiers from planes as "a turkey shoot." The look of glee in his eyes, the excitement in his voice, while he described spraying frightened men with high-caliber bullets from thousands of feet above them numbed me to the center of my soul. If truth were known, it confused me, too. After all, it was a good thing, wasn't it, that we had "won" a war with "so little bloodshed."

Then I read a Sufi tale and came to understand where the numbness had come from: Once upon a time there was an old woman who used to meditate early on the bank of the Ganges. One morning, finishing her meditation, she saw a scorpion floating helplessly in the strong current. As the scorpion was pulled closer, it got caught in roots that branched out far into the river. The scorpion struggled frantically to free itself but got more and more entangled.

She immediately reached out to the drowning scorpion, which, as soon as she touched it, stung her. The old woman withdrew her hand but, having regained her balance, once again tried to save the creature. Every time she tried, however, the scorpion's tail stung her so badly that her hands became bloody and her face distorted with pain.

A passerby who saw the old woman struggling with the scorpion shouted, "What's wrong with you, fool! Do you want to kill yourself to save that ugly thing?"

Looking into the stranger's eyes, she answered, "Because it is the nature of the scorpion to sting, why should I deny my own nature to save it?" Then I understood the numbness. I saw that Reverence for Life is of the essence of humanity.

And that is what we have lost. We "defend" ourselves by threatening the globe and our own level of civilized humanness with it. We have chosen technological progress and financial profits over the needs of human beings. We have bartered the quality of our own souls; we live the denial of Reverence for Life.

But we have become a society of machines and business degrees, of stocks and bonds, of world power and world devastation, of what works and what makes money. We train our young to get ahead, our middle-aged to consume, and our elderly to be silent. We are sophisticated now. We live in stadiums, not galleries. We listen to rap music, not Mozart. We talk about ideas for getting ahead rather than about our ideas for touching God. We are miles from our roots and light-years away from our upbringings. We have abandoned the concerns of the civilizations before us. We have forsaken the good, the true, and the beautiful for the effective, the powerful, and the opulent. We have abandoned enoughness for the sake of consumption. We are modern. We are progressive. And we are lost.

So what do I believe in? What do I define as human? I believe in the pursuit of the spiritual, the presence to pain, and the sacredness of life. Without these, life is useless and humanity a farce.

To be human it is necessary to think again about what matters in life, to ask always why what it is to be human is to listen to the rest of the world with a tender heart and learn to live life with our arms open and our souls seared with a sense of responsibility for everything that is.

Without a doubt, given those criteria, we may indeed not live the "better life," but we may, at the end, at least have lived a fully human one.

Rupert Sheldrake

RUPERT SHELDRAKE, PH.D., is a biologist and author of *Seven Experiments That Could Change the World, The Presence of the Past,* and four other books. He is married, has two sons, and lives in London.

We know very little about the nature of our minds. They are the basis of all our experience, our mental and social life, but we do not know what they are. Nor do we know their extent.

The traditional view, found all over the world, is that conscious human life is part of a far larger animate reality. The soul is not confined to the head but extends throughout and around the body. It is linked to the ancestors, connected with the life of animals, plants, the earth, and the heavens; it can travel out of the body in dreams, in trance, and at death; and it can communicate with a vast realm of spirits—of ancestors, animals, nature spirits, beings such as elves and fairies, elements, demons, gods and goddesses, angels and saints. Christian versions of this traditional understanding were prevalent all over Europe throughout the Middle Ages and still survive in rural societies, for example in Ireland.

By contrast, for more than three hundred years the dominant theory in the West has been that minds are located inside heads. This theory was first propounded by Descartes in the seventeenth century. Descartes denied the old belief that the rational mind was part of a larger soul, mainly unconscious, pervading and animating the entire body. Instead, he supposed that the body was an inanimate machine. Animals and plants were machines, too, and so was the entire universe. In his theory, the realm of the soul shrank from nature into man alone and then in the human body contracted yet further into a small region of the brain, which Descartes identified as the pineal gland. The conventional modern theory is essentially the same, except for the fact that the supposed seat of the soul has moved a couple of inches, into the cerebral cortex.

This model of the contracted mind, confining the soul to the brain, is shared by both sides in the familiar, long-standing debate between dualists and materialists. Descartes himself, the prototype Cartesian dualist, regarded the mind and the brain as fundamentally different in nature yet interacting within the brain in an unknown manner. By contrast, materialists reject this dualist conception of a "ghost in the machine" and believe that the mind is nothing but an aspect of the mechanistic functioning of the brain, or else that it is an inexplicable "epiphenomenon," rather like a shadow, of the brain's physical activity. But although these rigorous materialistic views are espoused by some philosophers and ideologists, dualism is far more prevalent in our culture and is usually regarded as common sense.

In the older imagery of popular science, the machinery was controlled by little men inside the brain. In more up-to-date images, the machinery has been modernized, but the homunculi are still there, if only implicitly. For example, in a current exhibit in the Natural History Museum in London titled Controlling Your Actions, you can find out how you work by looking through a Perspex window in the forehead of a model man. Inside is the cockpit of a modern jet plane, with banks of dials and computerized flight controls. There are two empty seats, presumably for you, the ghostly pilot, and your copilot in the other hemisphere. The currently fashionable computer metaphor for the brain is no different: if the brain is the hardware and habits and skills the software, then you are the phantom programmer.

How many people really think of themselves as a machine? Even ardent materialist philosophers and mechanistic scientists do not seem to take this belief very seriously, at least in relation to themselves and their loved ones. In personal as opposed to official life, most people still retain to varying degrees the older and broader perspective of their ancestors. First, the soul is often thought to pervade more of the body than the brain. And second, the soul is widely believed to participate in extended psychic and spiritual realms, stretching far beyond the confines of the body.

In Hindu, Buddhist, and other traditional psychologies, there are several animating centers within the body, the *chakras*, each with its own characteristic properties. In the West, too, various psychic centers have traditionally been recognized, in addition to the head. For example, people often talk of "gut feelings." And although from a mechanistic point of view the heart is just a pump, expressions such as "heartfelt thanks," "heartless behavior," and "warmhearted-ness" obviously refer to more than a blood-pumping mechanism. So does the heart as a symbol of love. Indeed, our ancestors believed that the focus of psychic life was in the heart, not the brain. The heart was more than a center of emotion, love, and compassion; it was a center of thought and imagination, just as it still is for many traditional peoples today, including the Tibetans. Think, for example, of the phrases still used in Christian liturgy, in the Magnificat: "He hath scattered the proud in the imagination of their hearts" and in the Collect for Purity in *The Book of Common Prayer*: "Almighty God, unto whom all hearts be open, all desires known and from whom no secrets are hid, cleanse the thoughts of our hearts by the inspiration of thy Holy Spirit."

The old sense of the psyche as extended beyond the limits of the body is also widespread in our culture. This is implied in common turns of phrase such as "your ears must have been burning yesterday, because we were talking about you." It is also implied by telepathy and other psychic phenomena. In Britain, the USA, and other Western countries, surveys have repeatedly shown that a substantial majority of the population believe in their occurrence and more than 50 percent claim to have personal experience of such phenomena.

Such experiences and beliefs do not make sense if the mind is confined to the brain, nor if all communication depends on the known principles of physics. For these reasons, defenders of mechanistic orthodoxy often assert that since "paranormal" phenomena cannot be scientifically explained, they cannot exist. Belief in them is regarded as a superstition, to be eradicated through scientific education.

What started as a radical philosophy has now become the orthodox doctrine of our culture, picked up in childhood and thereafter taken for granted. According to the classic studies of Jean Piaget on the mental development of European children, by the age of about ten or eleven most children have learned what he calls the "correct" view, namely, that thoughts are located inside the head. By contrast, younger children believe that they travel outside their bodies when they dream; that they are not separate from the living world around them but participate in it; that thoughts are in the mouth, breath, and air; and that words and thoughts can have magical effects at a distance. In short, European children show the animalistic attitudes that are found in traditional cultures all over the world and which were prevalent in our own culture until the mechanistic revolution.

However, Cartesian theory of an immaterial mind within a machinelike brain ran into serious problems from the outset. By equating the soul with the rational mind, Descartes denied the bodily and unconscious aspects of the psyche, previously taken for granted. Ever since Descartes, the unconscious psyche has had to be reinvented. For example, in 1851 the German physician C. G.

Carus wrote a treatise on the unconscious which began as follows: "The key to an understanding of the nature of the conscious life of the soul lies in the sphere of the unconscious.... The life of the psyche may be compared to a great, continuously circling river which is illuminated in only one small area by the sun."

Through Sigmund Freud's work, the recognition of the unconscious became widespread among psychotherapists; and in Carl Jung's notion of the collective unconscious the psyche is no longer confined to individual minds but shared by everyone. It includes a kind of collective memory in which individuals participate unconsciously.

There has also been a growing awareness in the West of Indian, Buddhist, and Chinese traditions, all of which offer a richer understanding of the relation of the psyche to the body than the mechanistic theory. And through explorations of the effects of psychedelic drugs, the visionary practices of shamans, and Oriental techniques of meditation, the existence of other dimensions of consciousness has become a matter of personal experience for many Westerners.

Thus, although the confining of the mind to the head of a machinelike body is still orthodox in mechanistic science and medicine, it coexists with survivals of an earlier and broader understanding of the psyche. It is also subject to the articulate and sophisticated challenges posed by Jungian and transpersonal psychology, psychical research and parapsychology, mystical and visionary traditions, and holistic forms of medicine and healing.

Janis Roze

One day shortly after World War II, I was walking across the ruins of a bombed-out part of Freiburg in southern Germany. Several city blocks were nothing but rubble. A few small pathways were zigzagging through the destroyed city quarter, otherwise devoid of life and people. Then I suddenly stopped in wonder. Surging from the piles of bricks and stones there was a single tree fearlessly reaching up from this scene of devastation.

Life is stronger than human destructiveness! I turned around, rushed back to the university where I, a Latvian refugee of the war, was studying, and changed my major to biology. I was to become a herpetologist, an expert in

JANIS ROZE is a professor of biology at the City University of New York. Roze is an author and lecturer who has worked with the American Museum of Natural History and the United Nations Center of Science and Technology for Development. For many years he has worked as an editor for ICIS Forum: An Instrument for Human Dialogue on Important Contemporary Issues and Problems and on the Future of Humanity.

snakes. I wanted to know about this power of life. The tree was growing in a seemingly impossible environment. I had to learn about this tree and all other living beings and to find out if humans also have this magic power to transcend the "rubble of human society" produced by the horrors of war, destructiveness, violence, arrogance, separateness, insensitivity, and sheer inhumanity that I learned about and lived with during the six years of war. I had to discover the magic of living being demonstrated by this Phoenix-like rebirth of "my" ailanthus tree.

What makes people who have seen the inhumanity and barbarism of war—it is still not transcended—press on, strive to be "better human beings," to think about the future, to stand for sharing and caring? Whence comes the power that enables so many to play a different game, constructively, heroically to keep hope alive, and trust and faith, and gives them the courage to wonder and— greatest wonder—to love?

I kept wondering about the uncanny ability of living organisms to grow, change, evolve, and never give up. Like humans, it is rooted in a common denominator of all life: Every individual organism has an inherent urge to survive, from bacteria to elephants and humans, yes, especially humans, where it is built into I-consciousness. As a human individual, I will fight to the last to survive as an "I world," because it is the only world that I am aware of, a complete universe in itself. My complete universe, moreover, is special and unique. I care about it because I have a sense that my life is going somewhere, that something important has to be accomplished. It seems that from the inherent urge to survive as an individual, the intriguing sense that I will live forever, blossom such uniquely human qualities as hope, trust, faith.

This sense of "something important to accomplish" seems to be a human characteristic. It is always there and emerging from the unconscious animal world. In humans this conscious "My life is going somewhere" is seen in the child's groping, in students' organizing their education, in professionals' building their future life, in artists' creating their art, in almost everything humans do.

Is it possible that, in spite of appearances, we have matured enough to discover something more and take the next step to humankind? In deciphering the "way of chaos" and the exquisitely abstract geometric nature of chaos, we are opening up a new perception of how this world and humankind function. As we are learning more about chaos, it is becoming apparent that every system, every movement, every action influences and relates everything to everything else, from local situations to humans, to the entire earth, and, indeed, to the universe. We realize that, almost magically, beneath the surface of fragmentation and barbarism our own separateness is dissolved by the wholeness of the earth. One conclusion of this is that the flow of human life is totally interdependent with the living and nonliving world as equal partners.

Years later studying the ecology of the *arrau*, a river turtle, on a Venezuelan island in the Orinoco River, I was offered a glimpse of the great interdependence, or inner coherence of all that is. For two weeks I was living alone, studying the ecology of the river turtle, far away from any human settlement. Aloneness, the hot sand beach, the rhythm of the gently flowing river, the day-and-night company of some seventeen thousand females laying eggs, and my own presence burst into my awareness as one whole picture. In that magical sunset, we all melted into the flow of events, without time. I "saw" the emergence of sand and river several billion years ago, pushing ahead. With evolution going somewhere, they offered themselves for the whisper of life: plants with their green magic of feeding themselves from the sun. Then I "saw" the earth in another creative burst out of the existing manifestation molding the animal world. The turtles, crocodiles, and capuchin monkeys of my island company were living proof of this push. But the work was not finished, and I, the human, emerged from this flow of life, holding in my amazed consciousness the continuation of all this enormous evolutionary whole. At that moment, not very much of me was left, except an intense awareness of the powerful stream of existence in which everything formed One Whole of which I was a part.

There was an enormous surge of wonder about all that existed, a participatory respect for everything in which I and not-I at the same time were included. Yes, a respect for what life has blessed me with and the uncanny realization that I was part of a continuum embracing all that is. In the soft air of the Orinoco sunset, my mind-heart uttered an unspoken realization of a deep Reverence for Life because it was the thread leading to eternity. Was it the Reverence for Life, for any life, felt by Albert Schweitzer in his confrontation with African nature and humans? Was it a recognition and Reverence for Life of a Thomas Berry that includes the living and the nonliving world as equal partners? That and perhaps an all-encompassing awe for the whole of existence, of that incomprehensible creation that pulsates in every atom, rock, fern, ant, and human.

The Time of the Human has reached a point at which either we become aware of belonging to, of our being a manifestation of, the One Whole or we shall perish proclaiming that we individually and as a species are an exclusive fragment of the Great Separateness. The Christ's challenge is to redeem separateness and temporarity, to overcome it in timelessness, in that Christ consciousness that is fully Human.

Willem A. M. Alting von Geusau

I see myself again as a lanky Franciscan monk in a brown habit. It was in 1967 and I had twelve years of experience as what one could call a choirmaster of the wholesale variety, a crowd manipulator actually. I had become a virtuoso at it. I merely had to lift my arms, open my mouth, and a few thousand throats started to jubilate as if with one single hugely amplified voice.

WILLEM A. M. ALTING VON GEUSAU is a self-made generalist who was a Franciscan monk and pastor for twenty-seven years and has been an educational psychologist in the vocational training programs of general practitioners for more than twenty-two years.

The week before there had been fifteen thousand schoolchildren at a Mass on the city square of Maastricht. Then came the day that in Utrecht, at the end of a Pax Christi pilgrimage, four thousand mortals—in this case students—sat on their backpacks in a huge hall. I stood on the podium to the left of the altar that had been built there for the Mass which His Eminence was going to celebrate. And so I lifted my right arm, did the required minor gesturing with my left one, and those thousands of voices exploded in songs about peace, about a better world to come, and, of course, about Jesus. The TV cameras swiveled from His Eminence to me, to the mass of kids who suddenly took the initiative and started to bellow, "He is a jolly good fellow." The cardinal produced a wide grin, trusting me to keep the outburst within limits of piety.

Of course, knowing how to handle such crowds, I only had to wave both arms to succeed brilliantly. But then, when it was all over, I disappeared backstage and almost vomited. I felt deadly ashamed, miserable. So I could manipulate a crowd, even a mob, but so could Hitler, and we know what resulted from that, all the way to Auschwitz. I swore: never again, never, never again. It was a turnabout. At one stroke, liberated from all those years of monastic imprisonment, I knew the time had come to switch from mass manipulation to focus on the human individual, to start becoming human myself, to respect what is human in others.

After twenty years in a Franciscan brown habit, I see myself suddenly in jeans, in Kansas, at the Menninger Foundation, Department of Religion and Psychiatry. I was forty by now, working with young criminals of the Boys Industrial School, meanwhile learning what it is to look into oneself, to be really involved with others, to feel intimacy, compassion, suffering, to participate in the suffering of others, instead of distributing the patented formulas of "neighborly love."

Now, at sixty-seven, having switched long ago from churches and big auditoriums to the little room where I sit face-to-face with individual humans, it remains my daily exercise to resist all temptation to categorize, to label socially, politically, professionally, religiously the one opposite me, simply recognizing the human being, hence capable of empathy, compassion, foresight, and trusting their specific humanness. For I believe in the sanity at the core of every human being, equipped with the humanizing functions of the prefrontal cortex: insight, empathy, sympathy, compassion, and foresight that give us the ability to become fully human, to transcend the devastating automatisms of our conditioning, liberating our creative energies in our reactions to ourselves and to others.

I believe in a new approach to health care which recognizes the sick person as a unique human being, on the basis of a consciousness of the physician and other givers of health care of a shared uniqueness as human individuals.

I also believe that the traumatic experiences of individual or collective violence are part of our human condition and that as victims of such violence we are often able to liberate ourselves by means of our innate sanity from obsessive negative feelings toward those who inflicted suffering on us. I feel that the cultivation of the "victimization" of Jesus, together with the denial of the meaning of the Resurrection, has generated throughout the centuries those obsessive negative feelings toward the Jews, as the seed from which Auschwitz could grow.

To affirm the Self, the "godly" in us, without losing our unique identity is what Schweitzer's Reverence for Life means to me in its simplicity, its all-including poignancy.

Willem A. M. Alting von Geusau   165

Chungliang Al Huang

CHUNGLIANG AL HUANG is a performing artist and internationally acclaimed Tao master. He is the author of the best-selling classic *Embrace Tiger, Return to Mountain* and coauthor with Alan Watts of *Tao: The Watercourse Way*.

In 1937, when I was still in my mother's womb, the Chinese government sent my father to America as an envoy to voice its concerns about the Japanese invasion and to seek international support for China's plight.*

My mother, eight and a half months pregnant, and our entire three-generation family she headed during Father's absence, including my four siblings, ages two to six, barely escaped the brutal "Nanjing Massacre," to seek sanctuary in Shanghai for my birth.

---

*In December 1937, Nanjing fell to the Japanese Imperial army. The Japanese army launched a massacre that lasted six weeks. According to the records of several welfare organizations which buried the dead bodies after the massacre, around three hundred thousand people, mostly civilians and POWs, were brutally slaughtered.

The Japanese then began bombing that terror-stricken port city and forced the hospital where my mother was in labor to evacuate and suspend normal functions. My grandmother, a fragile Mandarin lady with bound feet, had to summon all her strength and intuitive feminine know-how to deliver me in the deserted, collapsing hospital.

Twelve days later, our family cowered aboard the refugee ship SS *Hunan* bound for Hong Kong. A typhoon struck halfway out on the China Sea, annihilating most of the passengers. By the grace of God, our family survived and was rescued. We eventually managed to hide in small villages in southern China to evade the expansion of the Japanese occupation, through eight long years of isolation and struggle.

My memories of these early years are filled with a fusion of untainted rural beauty, kindhearted peasants, with air raids and abrupt relocations often in the depth of night. Idyllic summer afternoons spent barefooted in the patchwork of rice paddies, climbing on the slippery, muddy backs of water buffaloes in the rain, helped to soothe my nightmares of bombings and the sudden absences of schoolmates and friends killed. For me, it seemed natural and was psychologically necessary to grow up balancing these contrasting experiences that became the foundation for my faith and optimism in humanity and life.

After the war we managed a few brief years of peace and settlement but then again were refugees, frantically escaping from the dangerous chaos of the Nationalist/Communist unrest in China. From Nanjing, the Nationalist capital, we were forced to flee south to the very edge of the mainland, then, once again in the middle of the night, rushed to an air base, strapped into military aircraft, and relocated on Taiwan. Left behind forever were all our valuables, generations of family treasure.

Looking back, after nearly half a lifetime in America, I am grateful to have weathered the terrors of my youth, clearly aware of my good fortune in having been able to migrate West to have become a world citizen during a new life that forced me to balance both Eastern and Western influences. My life's work has allowed me to reenter deeper into my Chinese heritage, and to share my ancestral cultural riches with the world.

In spite of the inhuman atrocities, my experience confirmed that mankind shares a moral spirit that generates and inspires kindness and compassion. In all primal cultures, human beings felt identified with universe and community. "Self"-consciousness was a much later development in human evolution. In China, 2,500 years ago, Lao-tzu and Chuang-tzu taught us to get out of our small self, to reenter into cosmic consciousness. Confucius and Mencius taught that there was good in all of us, that we need to cultivate these virtues, to look for and reinstill the humanity in ourselves which went astray, and that cooperatively we can and will be able to revisualize and rebuild a harmonious future world.

An example of this human-heartedness (the Chinese symbol is *JEN*, which illustrates a "giving and receiving" relationship between two human beings) is in this story from the 1991 great flood of the Yangtze River. While people from the northern cities were amassing truckloads of warm bedding and winter clothes to rush south, an elderly retired soldier stripped off his only cotton-quilted old coat and tossed it into the pile. Not until the following day did he remember that he had also given away his entire life's savings, secretly sewn into the lining of his coat.

Weeks later, while the soldier despaired at the thought of trying to survive the frigid Beijing winter, the southern man who had received the coat suddenly discovered the hidden money. Realizing how devastated the original owner must be, he set out north to find his benefactor. Not knowing how to trace the anonymous donor, he began telling everyone along the path about the heroic deed. Soon the media spread the story, and the happy ending ensued when the two met and the money was returned. All of China was cast in a heartwarming glow.

Global consideration may need to begin with just such a "ripple effect"—as a small pebble dropped in a pond creates endless concentric circles. How we relate to ourselves determines how we relate to others. By cultivating the best in ourselves, we begin to offer the possibility of change, change that comes from the individual heart and ripples outward, creating a unified, interconnected global community with those who are different, those we don't understand. We will then see how, in our differences, we are all linked.

Jacques Langlais

JACQUES LANGLAIS, C.S.C., PH.D., is the founder of the Intercultural Institute of Montreal, devoted to research and education in the field of cross-cultural relations. He is the author of numerous writings on major intercultural topics.

If you ask me what being a human means to me, two memories come to mind:

The first goes back to a journey to Asia in the spring of 1962. I was on my way to visit a friend I had known in university who was living with his family in the vicinity of Vellore in South India. I arrived by bus from Madras, after sunset, with no reservation for the night. Loaded with two suitcases, I started looking for shelter. The streets were already deserted. All signs were in Tamil: no English version, no Latin script. I might as well have been illiterate. I was about to lose heart when I saw a light beaming from a basement. Through the window, I could see some twenty young men attending a lecture, all eyes glued on their professor. The walls were covered with an unusual combination of pictures: Hindu gods side by side with Jesus, the Blessed Virgin, and a few Christian saints. Feeling reassured, I ventured to the doorway. I was wearing traditional Western clerical dress. Upon seeing me, the teacher dismissed his students and came to me. He spoke English. He readily understood my situation. All hotels and inns were full. An important conference was taking place in town, he said. He brought me to a kind of restaurant where I was served a tasty meal on a banana leaf. As I ate, I noticed him conversing at length with the manager. He then came back to tell me there was a bed for me upstairs.

At dawn the next morning, I left my little room to catch the bus and continue my journey. To my astonishment, as I opened the door I saw a man wrapped in a blanket sleeping on the veranda floor. Careful not to wake him, I left, realizing he had given up his place to the exhausted traveler that I was. Thus, beyond the differences of our religious and cultural worlds, I had been granted the privilege of a threefold hospitality, thanks to the kindness of the teacher, the inn's manager, and an unknown guest in a small town of the Indian subcontinent. I never again met these three men, nor did I learn more about them except that they were human in the full sense of the word.

MY OTHER RECOLLECTION IS MORE RECENT. It goes back to the 1990 casino crisis in Akwesasne. Akwesasne is a Mohawk reservation located on the shore of the Station Lawrence River and straddling the borders of New York State, Ontario, and Quebec. The Warriors were running seven casinos there, which attracted busloads of gamblers from cities as far off as Pittsburgh, Toronto, Montreal, and Ottawa. In order to stop this invasion, which wrecked life on the reservation, the Akwesasne population of traditional bent set up blockades at both ends of the village east and west. The Warriors retorted by sending the spiritual chief of the Mohawks, Sakokwenionkwas, an ultimatum. Should the blockades still be there at eight o'clock that same evening, they would be torn down by force.

Sakokwenionkwas immediately called upon friendly groups beyond the reservation, including pacifists from Montreal, Ottawa, and New York City. In response to this appeal, the Intercultural Institute of Montreal, represented by my colleague Robert Vachon and myself, decided to join the peace delegation. At sunset Sakokwenionkwas performed the ritual of spreading sweetgrass ashes on the blockades. I then found myself with a party that was sent to the eastern end of the Akwesasne to the Saint Regis River bridge. At the appointed time, we saw two huge bulldozers coming toward us side by side. They stopped halfway over the bridge. It was the Warriors with their AK-47s. The people present had moved forward, unarmed, led by young couples forming a human chain, singing Martin Luther King's famous "We Shall Overcome."

At that point a dialogue worthy of Greek tragedy took place between the two parties. Addressing a Clan Mother who was probably a relative, a Warrior said, "You had better let us pass. Aren't you afraid to die?"

"It's easy to kill me," was the answer, "but remember, I have five children and you'll have to take care of them if I go."

This confrontation between brute force and moral strength lasted several long minutes when suddenly a miracle happened. The huge machines were put in reverse and withdrew. This population, tragically divided between the supporters of gambling and intimidation and the guardians of the Great Law of Peace of the Iroquois Nations, had just shown itself to be deeply human. The Warriors had responded to a cry from the heart of a mother.

These two life experiences confirmed my conviction that being human is not the monopoly of any one culture, different as it may be from mine. In our Western languages, the word *barbarian* is synonymous with the word *savage* from the Latin *silva*, forest, with the consequence that the foreigner and the forest dweller are equated in the mind of the "civil-ized," the city-man (*civis*). In ancient Rome, the "barbarian" and the "savage" were kept beyond the lines, beyond the borders, of the empire. They were a permanent threat to the space governed by the *lex romana*.

But is, in reality, the "civilized" free from violence, cruelty, and behaviors threatening to civilization? Who invented bacteriological warfare, nuclear arms, the "final solution," and so many other crimes against mankind? Essentially, what makes one's action inhuman is not to act like a beast; it is to act against what makes us human. The human family will end up either in accepting itself totally or in disappearing. In this sense—and insofar as they remain faithful to their original inspiration—the great educators of humanity, the religious and cultural traditions, are still our best guarantee of survival, provided these traditions avoid the trap of those who want to turn them into war machines at the service of their personal crusades.

Ludek Broz

LUDEK BROZ is professor emeritus of systematic theology in Prague. He is an author, editor, and publisher of *Metanoia Press,* an ecumenical quarterly.

In one of Fellini's films a young filmmaker—played by Mastroianni—successful but troubled, looks to a grim old cardinal for advice. Their meeting takes place in a steamy Turkish bath, both wrapped in nothing but their bath sheets. "You see, Your Eminence, I am not happy," the film director begins. The cardinal looks at him for a very long second and croaks, "And why do you think you should be?"

Fellini once again points at the contrariety between our materialistic-nihilistic practice and the vague but irrepressible remnants of Christian, or any ethical/religious, values that make us whine in all tonalities, "We are not happy," provoking the counterquestion: "And why should we be?"

It challenges the Euro-American dogma of our entitlement to happiness we are urged to pursue. Every ad, in print or on TV, whether commercial or political, urges: "You will be deliriously happy and forever, if you buy! Buy our new new!! dishwasher, our unisex skin lotion, our cholesterol-free mutual fund! our spiritual bingo!" Still, it is becoming extremely difficult to combine being human and happy in a world of car bombs, Gulf Wars, Rwanda, Cambodia genocides, Srebrenica's subanimal barbarism. I have some difficulty being blissfully happy with all those wretched slums in our rich North while the stock markets hit the ceiling.

It takes extraordinary callousness to be happy in a Global Village where a microminority owns 60 percent of the land and 90 percent of the power supplies; where a huge majority is chronically hungry because of acutely exacerbated and engineered famine, combined with pursuing happiness and being human on our Free Market Square dominated by friendly transnationals that market missiles at bargain prices and cover the globe with nonstop, obscene sado-thrillers.

Whatever Fellini's cardinal has in mind, his pitiless rejoinder points at the Happiness Syndrome as the psychopathology of our neobarbaric "culture." Still I happen to believe that our world system, based on unadulterated greed, megamoney, megapower, and megacommunication, cannot be blamed exclusively on politicians, civil servants, and statesmen. Some of these people, even if they are committed to social justice, peace, and the well-being of humans, are held captive by constituencies infected with the Happiness Syndrome, so that conferences on life-and-death problems are bound to offer nothing but fictional aid to the Third World and lullabies dismissing the ever-threatening nuclear catastrophe. It would interfere with our pursuit of happiness that makes us so chronically unhappy.

There are nine points in a sermon the Rabbi of Nazareth once preached on the Mount that might act as wonder drugs against our Happiness Syndrome. I won't repeat them here, for this is not a preachment. Still, it is interesting to note that each one of these nine points starts with: "Blessed are they . . ." Consulting my French

Bible, I find that *blessed* is here translated as *heureux*, which means "happy." For instance: "Happy are they who are merciful, for they shall obtain mercy."

Fellini's cardinal might well smile this time: "And why do you think they shouldn't be?"

Pedro Aznar

Thus Far

This is what I have seen
thus far:
Everybody, stronghold of
     "mine that will never be
yours nor ours":
uncontrollable fear: blind fear
of opening the door, letting
one another see
we are naked;
countless processions
running after ideal love, phantasm that always
dissolves, always,
as it turns the corner;
fruitless inventions of every type and sort
to convince ourselves that happiness can be anything else but
surrender to the other;
rules, precepts, theories, useless credos (principles?)
for they do not include the soul.

PEDRO AZNAR is an
Argentine musician, composer,
and poet. He is the winner of
three Grammy awards for his
recordings with the Pat Metheny
Group.

that soul blessed for rejecting imprisonments;
they are the Olympus of the fools who believe in arriving-somewhere
by banishing love
as the indefinable;
multitudes of hypocrites stoning those who show
their empty hands;
pessimists without motive;
optimists without reason;
whatever-ists mounting the next available car,
distrust, nourished by knowing the other
conceals the same monsters within;
hate, born from blindness to the monsters
in ourselves;
shaping humans in the image and likeness
of perverse gods, vengeful and ignorant;
separation, separation everywhere;

this is not that, not the other

nor that which lies beyond, painful price
of loneliness;
in the schools, the dead throwing barren dirt
on the divine seed of childhood;
impotent and petty nudgings of parents
proclaiming themselves owners of their Sons of Life
(Life, which expects nothing from anyone!);
those who want everything to stay as it is
looting with screams, bullets or shame
the gifts of youth;
So vast an ocean of pain
when everything could be so different!

I have also seen
the ones who do not give up

searching blindly

holding on to, or letting go of, a center in the changing tides;

leaving in the furious winds a tenuous track of unmistakable
perfume;

every day, fighting the most crucial battles, the only noble ones,
within

erasing with blood the dark commandments (one's own
or those of others);

going astray, losing one's way and starting anew;

doubting one's strength yet baring one's chest;

knowing that all is still to be done, has to be done by everyone
every time;

testing one's courage in the blackness of the darkest night.

Satish Kumar

SATISH KUMAR is editor of the journal *Resurgence* in London and founder of the Schumacher College in Devonshire.

My first memory of my life was seeing the dead body of my father when I was four years old. It was a moving, touching, confusing, bewildering, perplexing moment. I could not understand what had happened to my father, and I could not understand why everybody was crying. When I later saw my father's body being burned and heard my mother say that I would never see him again, I became unsettled. And I asked myself, "Is there any way that one can stop people from dying?" Although intellectually I could not analyze the situation, I felt intuitively that there must be a way to overcome death, so that people don't cry, so people don't look sad. That led me on a long quest.

The second most important event in my life was my mother's death. It was something quite extraordinary, because my mother did not die suddenly like my father. At this time I was forty-five. My mother was old, about eighty, and one day she said to us, "I'm now too old; I can't cook; I can't do anything for you. What point is there in carrying on? From tomorrow, I'm going to start dying."

We were amazed. But she went around the village seeing her friends, her relatives, her children, her grandchildren, people who had worked with her, saying, "I have come to say good-bye because I am going to die." Then she started to fast until death and lay peacefully. People sang hymns, songs, chants, mantras, and prayed and meditated for her good voyage into the next life. I have never experienced a celebration of death in such a beautiful way, and it allowed me to come to terms with the idea of death more clearly.

Before that, however, I was in quest of knowing about life. Until I could understand what life is, I could not understand what is death. So I became a monk—a Jain monk because Jain monks promised me that the only way to end the cycle of death and birth is to be free from this world and free from this body through spirituality. For nine years I followed that path as a monk. It was a beautiful experience.

One day I read in the news that a great English philosopher, Sir Bertrand Russell, was sent to jail because he was protesting against nuclear weapons. Here was a man of ninety, frail, ready to die, yet he went to jail for his convictions, his beliefs, for peace and the well-being of everybody in the world. And here I was, a young man, sitting here comfortably, drinking coffee and enjoying life. That gave me a shiver and I could not sleep that night.

A close colleague and I decided that we should go to support Russell and help this movement. We would walk from India to Moscow, Paris, London, and Washington, D.C.—four nuclear capitals of the world—and protest against these weapons. Our teacher and guru said, "It is a beautiful idea to experience the world, communicate with people, and go walking around the world for peace. I would like to give you two weapons of protection, like armor. One is that you go without any money in your pockets. And the second is that you remain a vegetarian, whatever the circumstances."

I was puzzled. I could understand being a vegetarian. But without money, how could we go around the world? Sometimes we might need a cup of tea. Sometimes we would need to write a postcard or make a phone call. Our teacher said, "No. You have to have trust in people if you are working for peace. The whole reason that we have wars in the world is because people don't trust. So when you practice trust you will not be walking for peace; you will be peace, the embodiment of peace. If you have money, you will walk all day. You will arrive in a town or village. You will go to sleep in a bed in a hotel. You will eat in a restaurant. You will meet nobody, or very few. But if you have no money, you will be forced to find some kind, generous family or person to give you hospitality for the night. When they give you hospitality and give you food, you will say you are vegetarian and they will ask why. Then you can talk about peace. Peace with nature, peace with animals, peace with soil, peace with rivers and mountains. The attitude which allows human beings to kill animals to satisfy their tastes, to destroy forests, to poison the soil is the same attitude that leads to war, because it is the attitude of exploitation for self-interest."

So began a walk that took eighteen months and covered eight thousand miles. It was a tremendous experience of being one with the earth, walking upon the earth, touching the earth every day with our feet. It gave me a great, deep reverence for the earth and for nature, and I realized that the earth is sacred. It was an eighteen-month-long earth meditation

It is now an accepted scientific fact that we are one living organism. So spirituality leads us from there and tells us that we are one living organism and we have to take care of one another. We cannot destroy. We are nature. We are earth, fire, water, air. We are time; we are space; we are consciousness. Environment is not out there, something separate from us.

This inspirational wisdom is not new. It is a perennial philosophy that is present in Confucianism, Taoism, the Indian philosophy where the whole of existence is one cosmic dance. It is in American Indian philosophy, where they say that the whole earth is one mother, grandmother earth and we are one family. Some members of the family have two legs. Some members have four legs. Some members have wings. Some members have branches. Some members bloom, like flowers. We are all one family.

But perennial philosophy has to be reinterpreted, reexperienced, and reexamined in our modern language. So now we know that the view of the whole earth as one living organism is proved by science. If they are destroying the rain forest in Brazil, they will be destroying the ozone layer over the whole planet without even knowing it. If they are producing air pollution in England, the trees will be affected in Sweden. If there is a nuclear accident in Chernobyl, the sheep and cows will be affected in Scotland. This is cyclical thinking, and it is new, and it is old. In a linear approach, you have a sort of progressive thought and you think everything new had nothing to do with the old. I don't believe in original thought. I believe in a cyclical way of thinking. And that means old ideas come in new language.

The difference between religion and spirituality is that religion is a form, an organization, to hold the value and the spirit. I sometimes use the image of a well. You have one well which is built with bricks. You have another well which is built with stone. You have another well which is 5 feet in diameter. You have a well which is 40 feet deep, another which is 100 feet deep.

These are the shapes and forms of different kinds of wells. But if you reach deep enough, the water is the same. So we need to look at Buddhism, Christianity, Islam, Hinduism, and a number of other religions as holding the water of the spirit. We must not get hooked on the shape and the form of the well. We are saying, "My well is better than your well. My well is deeper than your well. My well is bigger than your well."

My purpose in changing consciousness is to point out that if you go deep and drink the water of the spirit, then you will have your thirst quenched. Otherwise, you will remain thirsty and will go on quarreling.

At the moment, human society is on a path where we have forgotten that enough is enough and how much is enough. As a result, the single occupation of modern civilization is the unending, unlimited pursuit for more and more material possessions, a higher and higher living standard, more and more economic growth. A Chinese proverb says that when a human being or a society or a community or a nation does not know when enough is enough, however much they have, they will never have enough; but when a human being or a community or a nation or a society knows when enough is enough, they will realize that they already have enough.

I believe humanity is at the turning point. We are at the threshold of a new change. The millennium that is ending and the new millennium that is starting might be a good focal point. We are at a time when people are realizing that enough is enough, that we cannot go on being greedy, destroying the resources of the earth. Environment, ecology, our relationship with the earth, are going to become a strong catalyst for a transformation of our consciousness. I see it happening all around the world. More and more people are prepared to talk about the place of the spirit. More and more people are talking about matters of the soul. Young people particularly are becoming concerned about how we can stop the destructive practices we are engaged in.

So I have great hope. I believe we have reached a sort of peak of the industrial, technological, materialistic paradigm. We are at the point when new ideas and new approaches are emerging. But we have to remember that this industrial society was built over hundreds of years. We cannot have a transformation into a new paradigm overnight. We need patience.

Joanna Macy

I believe that we humans can destroy our world. I do not mean the annihilation of our planet, which is hardly dependent on one species or on any other single strand in its manifold matrix of life. I mean that we can provoke the collapse of our civilization and the ecological balance and variety necessary to any civilization, to life-forms complex enough for self-reflective consciousness, for aeons to come.

JOANNA MACY, PH.D., is a scholar of Buddhism, general living systems theory, and deep ecology. She is the author of several books, including *World as Lover, World as Self, Mutual Causality, Dharma and Development,* and *Mutual Development.*

Due to our ignorance and immaturity in combination with unprecedentedly powerful technologies, we are now in the process of actually accomplishing such wholesale destruction. Technology amplifies, accelerates, and compounds the intentions of its users and becomes highly toxic when these intentions are shaped by fear and greed. To consume ourselves to death and waste our last hours in murderous conflict is not the only path open to us.

No generation in history has been in a position to play a more decisive role in the course of conscious life on Earth than we on the cusp of the twenty-first century. I believe that we are capable of waking up together to the peril and promise of the present global crisis. Such an awakening is fully within human capacity, because it is the nature of self-organizing systems to evolve through mutual cooperation for the sake of the larger whole. A freshly perceived and experienced relationship between ourselves and all beings can provide the necessary motivation and wisdom to dismantle the politico-economic structures impelling our suicidal behaviors. We need to see and sense, more clearly than ever before, our mutual belonging. Powerful natural dynamics come into play, once we choose to be fully present to our world and commit ourselves to its healing. The primary and essential step is an act of awareness: to become alive to our own experience and speak truth about what we see, feel, and know is happening to our world.

In truth we belong to one another like cells in a larger body, each of us intimately affected by the suffering of our people and planet; each experiences, at some level of awareness, pain for our world. Our survival depends on our acknowledging and respecting this pain for the world. It attests to our capacity to suffer-with, the literal meaning of compassion. When we know and speak the truth of our pain for the world, we open the cooperative feedback within the larger living system of which we are a part, essential for adaptive response.

Because we can feel pain with what befalls other beings in the web of life, we are an organic part of this web. We are members of the living body of Earth, branches on the same vine. As experiencers of compassion, we are what is known in the Buddhist tradition as *bodhisattvas*. The *bodhisattva* knows there is no private salvation, no point in standing aloof from this suffering world or trying to escape from it. We are in it together, like neurons in a neural net.

Not only do the great religions tell us this, but also systems theory and evolutionary biology. We belong to each other, as inter-woven strands within the same vast web. It is crucial to realize that our very uniqueness as individuals is a function of our interactions within this web. For only as living systems connect and interact are they able to differentiate, to flower in diversity of function and form. Disconnection is entropic, disorganizing into sameness and randomness, whereas the emergence of complexity and intelli-gence requires ever more intricate connections.

We have evolved in such systemic interdependence that each act on our part has repercussions within the larger web beyond our capacity to measure or even discern. Each choice we make can either tear at the fabric of life or serve to reweave it. It can either accelerate the entropic, disintegrative forces we have unleashed or counteract them by providing new linkages for life's self-organizing flows of energy and information.

The self-organizing flows within the web of life can empower and sustain the actions we take on its behalf. Their powers extend beyond the capacities and reaches of our separate, small, ego minds. In the ever more intricate neural net of connections that has brought us forth from rock and amoeba is a thrust of life for life, which wants to surge through us now for the continued flowering of life. Sometimes this thrust feels like an active intelligence that wants to think through us, in ever more elegant and inclusive pat-terns. Sometimes it seems more like a deep song that undergirds life and wants to keep on singing.

We can be expressions and conduits of the exquisitely self-orga-nizing powers of life. They represent to me the play of a great mind. Our own self-reflexive consciousness is the fruit of mind's unfolding. We can choose to give play to that larger mind in every act and choice we make.

Whether one is tending a garden, cooking in a soup kitchen, or organizing for the protection of old-growth forest, there is a sense of being sustained by something beyond our individual power, a sense of being acted "through." It is close to the traditional religious concept of grace yet distinct in that it does not require belief in a particular God or supernatural agency. One simply finds oneself empowered to act on behalf of other beings—on behalf of the larger whole—and the empowerment itself seems to come through that or those for whose sake one acts. In systems thinking it can be understood as synergy. I see it in operation all around me, not only in the persisting ever-fresh vegetation of Earth but also in the sprouting, grassroots citizen actions, solar energy technologies, and new ventures in community.

The beliefs I express provide me with no assurance about our chances for survival. They give me confidence, however, in the laws at work—or the mind at play—in the very structure of our universe. Weaving us together for ever-greater understanding and creativity, these laws are as generous and exacting as the blossoming of a lotus or the multi-beinged breathing of a rain forest. While I know that we humans of Earth may destroy our world, I also know it will not be because of satanic powers pitted against us or the essential meaninglessness of life. It will be because we will have failed in the way we receive the gift of life, failed in our love for ourselves and each other.

Stephen Hoe Snyder

I have maintained *zazen* practice for twenty years. I have studied with several teachers and communities. Ultimately I found each community to be repressing the essential human qualities and expressions. I have recently felt as though I were a lone voice in the crowd.

STEPHEN HOE SNYDER is a Buddhist lawyer in Northern California. He incorporates Buddhist ethics with the practice of law and teaches meditation and spiritual practices.

Your book allowed me to confirm my own validity as well as my opinion that treating one another as human benefits all.

It seems to me that as Westerners we typically emphasize the individual over the community. Our laws are designated and applied to give remedy to the individual "harmed" by society at large. In my view, taken to the extreme this attitude severs the thin connectors we share. The problem, of course, is as we separate from others, becoming more independent individuals, we remove the necessary opportunities to feel love. Both self-love and love for others are essential to our growth as individuals and as community. The independence we crave in the West is really the opposite of what we actually need. We seek to be so separated from others that we are safe, shielded from personal hurt. When we learn to open our hurt self, our repressed pain, we begin to be human. We begin to heal. With self-love we can heal and, when appropriate, open our love to others. This can offer others validation and safety as they open to their hidden pain—the pain of being human. Through openness to this suppressed pain we initiate a climate of honesty around us. We begin to truly speak the truth. Others intuitively know we express the truth and open themselves to us. These begin a process of healing together as community.

The isolated mystical state of enlightenment expressed by many modern teachers leaves no room for humanity. I have asked at various Zen centers, "How do we express humanity here?" My question goes unanswered and I was usually viewed as a crackpot.

One needs to drop the attachment to thinking of past history and future imagining. This allows one to "just be." When we can "just be" suchness is ever present. If asked what Zen is, I say it is seeing as nature sees itself.

Naomi Shihab Nye

Before you know what
    kindness really is
You must lose things,
feel the future dissolve in a
    moment
like salt in a weakened broth.
What you held in your hand,
what you counted and
    carefully saved,
all this must go so you know
how desolate the landscape
    can be
between regions and kindness.
How you ride and ride
thinking the bus will never stop,
the passengers eating maize and chicken
will stare out the window forever.

Before you learn the tender gravity of kindness,
you must travel where the Indian in a white poncho lies

NAOMI SHIHAB NYE is a poet,
novelist, and editor whose books
include *Red Suitcase* and *Words
Under the Words: Selected
Poems*. She has edited four
prizewinning anthologies of poetry
for young readers and was a
Guggenheim Fellow for
1997–98.

191

dead by the side of the road.
You must see how this could be you,
how he too was someone
who journeyed through the night with plans
and the simple breath that kept him alive.

Before you know kindness as the deepest thing inside, you
must know sorrow as the other deepest thing.
You must speak to it till your voice
catches the thread of sorrows
and you see the size of the cloth.

Then it is only kindness that makes sense anymore,
only kindness that ties your shoes
and sends you out into the day to mail letters and produce bread,
only kindness that raises its head
from the crown of the world to say
It is I you have been looking for,
and then goes with you everywhere
like a shadow or a friend.

John Grim

When I was young I leaned against the winds of North Dakota. If I long for that youth I am even more nostalgic for those winds. They move through all my memories of family affection, personal reflection, and troubled volition. Rising out of old glacial lakes, those winds carried the whooping cranes of my imagination into flight. Sometimes I would strip off my winter coat and intentionally sit out in the howling Dakota storms and defy the cold snow knowing that the winds would finally release me from my madness. Only the frozen bodies of the Arctic owls which my father had shot and placed in the garage knew more pain, I thought . . . how shortsighted my youthful assessment of that pain. How innocent my youthful

JOHN GRIM is a professor of religion at Bucknell University. A historian of religions, he undertakes annual field studies in American Indian lifeways among the Apsaalooke/Crow and the Swy-ahl-puh/Salish peoples. He published *The Shaman: Patterns of Religious Healing Among the Ojibway Indians.*

bravado in blissful ignorance of the reciprocities that empowered me and of the pathologies that fed my own aggrandizement.

What smokestack in what remote place stains the sky so that I might record these memories and thoughts on my computer? No barbarian shouts at the outer gates totally apart from myself. If I have slipped through the hourglass years, the whirling monster of these times, I have come face to face with myself. The antibarbarian statement has become a reflexive exercise in the tumultuous search through knowing the self and the other as one and two. I cannot cast an aspersion that does not return. I cannot imprison the demented madness away, but I can name it, speak it, remember it, celebrate it as a way now put aside. Love it even as I willfully let it go. Remembering and forgetting like the flapping wings of a great bird:

Across the sand hills the black-tipped
wings of the crane pierced
the years of my leave-taking
held me still.
deep, deep the indigo desires of Dakota youth
unfurled on the downy arms of the grasslands.
sough, sough through the hills beside the
ancient glacial lake
prairie winds sigh in the embrace.
wait, wait crimson storms
recall the first meeting
high plains lightning and savage flirtation.
now, now the spiked horns of sage caterpillars
mark my lips with the delicate patterns
of the liberated moth.
Traveling the roads where the people of friendship live,
hau kola! I hear the yearning earth
sing across the whirl of business
chasing the millennium
toward the emergence of an ecozoic age.

Arn Chorn-Pond

At various times Somdech Maha Gosananda, His Holiness the Dalai Lama, and Archbishop Tutu from Africa suggested that I should try to meditate. I should look forward to a more hopeful and brighter future. They were very sincere and compassionate

ARN CHORN-POND is a refugee from Cambodia who has worked with Judith Thompson's Children of War and is now a student in the United States.

with their suggestions. I felt their love and caring for everyone in the world, and for the earth itself. I have a great, profound respect for them individually and for their work, and for the message they give everywhere they go: peace on this earth. But for me it is not that easy to believe that human beings can live with one another. Even at this moment as I talk about it, my chest and my heart are filled with pain; I have a hard time breathing.

I couldn't sleep at night from the nightmares of my childhood in Cambodia. Not too long ago, in my country, hate, evil, greed, and thirst for power and blood took over. When the Khmer Rouge marched into our cities, towns, and districts in 1975 my world began to crumble right before my eyes. The Khmer Rouge started

195

to kill indiscriminately anyone associated, or having any connection, with intellect. They killed doctors, professors, students, artists. I was forced to live in a concentration camp which was once a Buddhist temple. The Khmer Rouge killed three times a day. I was ten years old when I was forced to watch people being slaughtered. I witnessed the murders of thousands of human beings, innocent human beings, before my eyes, including many members of my own family. Many times I was forced to be involved in the killing by taking off the victims' clothes or keeping them still. I was not allowed to cry, or they would kill me, too. I was confused; I had to make myself feel no pain for these victims. I saw women being raped and tortured and left to die on the spot. Babies were stuck with bayonets into their stomachs; their spleens were cut out when they were still alive. It was worse than any nightmare.

I can at least start to become a human being just like you all are and wish that children anywhere on this earth won't be forced to carry guns, to kill each other, and won't have to suffer anymore. Is this a foolish wish? Is it a foolish wish to have respect for the other's life as if it were my own?

In 1979 when the Vietnamese invaded Cambodia, the Khmer Rouge gave us guns and pushed us into the front line. Children who refused were shot in the head. Many of us ranged from eight [and] up, as long as we could carry guns. I was then about twelve. The Khmer Rouge would shoot us from behind if, against orders, we tried to leave the battleground. Thousands of children got shot to the left and right of me, many of them good friends. We carried guns made in China, America, Russia, so that we could kill others and each other, and they made profits out of it. I was one of the few lucky ones who survived that war at all.

I went crazy. I had to shut off all feelings, not to care. Life had lost all value.

Now I have a new home, a new family who love and care about me very much. Especially I have a very special sister, Judith Thompson, who persistently helps me and cares about me. She continues to see goodness in me. She refused to give up on me no matter what. This is true also of my new mom, Shirley, and I thank you so much, all of you who saved my life and who became permanently my role models in life. I grew to be a good person because of human beings like you and many others of my good friends who came into my life. Because of individual human beings like you who turned my life around, I refuse to die and I realize that life is more meaningful than death, that caring feels better than hate, and that giving is much more joyful than just taking or receiving.

What do I wish for the world to be? To have more human beings like you. Through what I have seen and experienced in the past, I don't think I can wish for any perfect world anymore, but I am scared to become adult myself.

James M. Mboje

JAMES M. MBOJE is a
Nigerian student at the City
University of New York, where he
is a member of the African Student
Association.

Growing up in Kenya, East
Africa, in a generation trapped
in uncertainties of creeds,
beliefs, and seemingly mean-
ingless traditions and cultures,
has been cruel but at the same
time very rewarding. My generation is born and grows up in
a postcolonial Africa, with no recollections of what used to be
except in stories and general reading, but we see and compare the
remnants of the colonial legacy and its institutions to our experiences in the new Africa.

My grandparents who were born before the establishment of the
colonial government were never caught in the culture of material-
ism or individuality and saw it as their primary responsibility,
whenever able, to fend for not only their immediate or extended
families but for the whole community. My grandfather was the
Very Reverend, a man of the church, but his charities cut across
religious boundaries. My other not very Christian grandparents, as
well as the pagan few who I grew up knowing, also shared the spirit

of seemingly endlessly giving to the wider community: a sense of genuine communalism that what is mine is also yours. This sense of all belonging, rich and poor, each responsible for the welfare of the larger society, was a continuity of African traditions.

My parents, the generation of the colonial process, embraced the Western idea of the nuclear family. It was a common lament to hear my mom exclaim what a pity we did not know our uncle so-and-so and other members of the wider family. The responsibilities of my parents rarely ventured outside their immediate family. As city dwellers, with different peoples of multiple ethnicities, they were more sympathetic than empathetic to the sufferings of others.

With the growth of modern and Western institutions, the struggle to provide for immediate members of one's family has caught up with everyone, and my parents personify the general attitudes of their generation. They gladly point a finger to the government and other groups but do not see it in themselves primarily to care for the unfortunate segments of our societies. In fact, it is not hard to detect a sense of animosity toward beggars, juvenile delinquents, and vagrants, as if they are somewhat responsible for their plights. We are becoming not more but less human!

Lukas van Witsen Franck

LUKAS VAN WITSEN FRANCK is a teacher and lecturer at the Seeing Eye Foundation.

As a child riding by the meadows of upstate New York, I wondered at those trees pushing their way through solid boulders in the fields. It was as if they could find what they needed to live in the heart center of a rock.

I was present when my mother died a few years ago. We had been fortunate, my mother and I, that a difficult relationship was given to right itself on the threshold of the "eternal," for as she lay dying she changed profoundly into who she really was, thereby teaching me very much.

The Death and Life of EveryOne is my father's contemporary variation on the medieval morality of *Everyman*. I am very familiar with it, for at one time or another I have played most of its roles over the last fifteen years. The most telling line of the play was to me the one spoken by Insight: "Wisdom is Life That Knows It Is Living."

In my mother's dying I saw it become manifest. I believe that she died in a sort of enlightened state, in awe of life and in love with it. She became the tree which, having pushed its way through the rock in the field, suddenly blooms. She embodied the EveryOne play's resolution in her dying, that potential for Insight that is indeed Human, the affirmation of the beauty and fragility of life, one's own and the other's, that leads to the compassion for all other life that is the Specifically Human.

In our era it is easy, all too easy, to be distracted. Technology fools us into thinking of ourselves as no more than computers, advertising tricks us into being no more than consumers, and entertainment distracts and leads ego into playing "tough" or "cool." Its omnipresent violence dulls our human capacity for compassion at these very moments when we need it most.

Wherever I look, I see that tree pushing through the hard soil and rock. In my work with blind people I see this struggle to live and thrive, and sometimes I see these blind ones burst into fully Human bloom. Now and then I feel privileged to help them in their struggle. How these people have managed to become who they are, to overcome so much and then flower, is difficult to say. Some were deeply religious Christians who seemed to live the Christian ideal of great compassion. Others were not "religious" at all.

I, for one, was raised without "religion," that is, without indoctrination in any religion. My father and Claske, my "stepmother," helped me to see, to appreciate, to wonder at things, to hold life sacred in all its forms. They in turn had been profoundly influenced by Albert Schweitzer, with whom they worked in Africa, and shared his "Reverence for Life." This was the ambience in which I grew up. Gulls and sandpipers, the horseshoe crabs at the seashore, my dog, cat, and hamster at home, the pigeons in the park were part of what they taught me to observe, to be part of. They infected me with their own joy and Reverence for Life.

As a student I worked in a nursing home, and I believe that this experience has helped me to both treasure life and constantly be aware of its finite nature. If I have any hope of becoming more fully Human, it is because of experiencing Reverence for Life. Few children are still exposed to the reality, the beauty, the fragility of living things. Their eyes glued to the screen, starved of the raw material of life, their emotions wither on the vine. There are sections in our cities where death is so omnipresent that those who survive are warped, their Specific Humanness impaired forever.

"May all see the Reality of Being before their end," is the blessing that ends my father's reflection in the play of *EveryOne*, on the meaning of being Human.

Richard Kiley

We can only revere what we
   know.
Contempt and indifference
   grope in darkness;
reverence is born of light.

RICHARD KILEY, actor and author, resided in Warwick, New York, until his death in 1999.

As a boy on my uncle's farm in
Michigan, I was a great hunter, loved killing whatever moved:
birds, rabbits, woodchucks, squirrels. I loved guns—the feel, the
smell, the power of them. But I remember the moment it stopped,
though it happened more than half a century ago. I even remember the very tree under which I was standing. I had shot a squirrel
out of that tree, saw it crashing down through the branches,
wounded, still alive. My shot had broken its back. I stood there
watching it struggle, and then it happened. It was as if a door suddenly opened in my head and a bright light flooded in that carried
with it an overwhelming shock of sorrow, shame, compassion,
regret.

   I put the squirrel out of its misery but never knowingly killed an animal again. Could that perhaps be the way evolution works—an impulse sparking across a portion of our brains as yet untouched, the dawning of a new awareness? If I could have said to that squirrel, "Sorry, but I need you for food," the shame might have been less. But to say, "I took your life to amuse myself . . ."

I believe that people who hunt for pleasure or sport are not evil; they are just asleep. Or their awareness must be blocked by vestiges of a once-justified hunting instinct, still surviving. It can't be a lack of "intelligence" in hunters. An Ernest Hemingway, a Theodore Roosevelt, were avid trophy gatherers, rationalizing their killing sport eloquently. Roosevelt must have had a change of heart or he might not have written later in life: "Whenever I hear of the extinction of a species, it is as though all the works of a great writer had perished."

Opposed as I am to hunting, I must confess I have full understanding for someone who kills a deer to feed his family but very little for one who leaves the deer to rot on the hillside and cuts off its head to mount it as a trophy in his den.

The riddle of which creature will die so that we may live is one we cannot solve with any certainty. Insofar as we still eat meat, we simply leave the killing to others and are accessories after the fact. We are beginning to realize that plants, too, have a degree of consciousness and every sip of water we swallow destroys millions of organisms. A tree was killed to supply the paper on which I am writing this.

As long as we walk this earth we will bring death in some form to other living things and some organism will one day (be it through disease, accident, or biological warfare) put an end to us. It is a matter of awareness and of compassion. When the American Indian killed to live he consciously honored the life. The real evil is not in the killing but in the callousness of taking life for pleasure, as a "sport," as "game." To speak of their flesh as "game" is an insult to the creatures so sacrificed.

Reverence for Life begins with awareness of life, from microcosm to the planet itself. We condemn ourselves unless we can hear nature's cosmic hymnody, listen to its music, and join in with the cosmic choir.

Harry M. Buck

HARRY M. BUCK was one of the founders of the American Academy of Religion and is executive editor of Anima Publications. He has taught history of religions at Wellesley College, the University of Pennsylvania, and the New School for Social Research.

When the twentieth century started with the opening salvos of World War I, there was unbounded optimism. "We won't come back 'til it's over over there," and then the world will be safe for democracy.

Where are we now, about to cross the fictitious line of a new century and a new millennium? Our media, our entertainment are corrupted by a neobarbarism, ignoring the works of dedicated humans who give their time, energy, and resources to the search for peaceful, supportive relationships. What do we still believe in? I can only answer for myself.

I BELIEVE in the intricate interdependence that maintains our world and in the revelation of power through a quickened understanding of the earth itself.

I BELIEVE in the lives and witness of a multitude of discerning and sensitive human beings in whom true selfhood and godhood are being realized: embodiments of the basic reality of the universe.

I BELIEVE in the universal sustaining strength by which all things were made that were made and by which all life is sustained.

This sustaining strength reveals itself not only through an appreciation of the life-giving energies we see throughout the world but also through fully realized humans. These manifestations are not confined to one people, one era, or one religious tradition.

We relate to others by labeling them with labels that have no reality; stereotypes we use for praise or blame: liberal/conservative, black/white, male/female, rich/poor, Christian/Jewish/Buddhist, and other such exclusionary terms. Just as I resist sticking labels on other humans, I refuse to apply such labels to myself, even though others may paste them on me.

I COMMIT MYSELF TO:

- vital participation—in time, energy and resources—with as many others as possible to foster the development of communities that value sustaining strength over dominating power;
- drinking the water of life from many wells, for no tradition or community can supply all my needs;
- the third step of the Buddha's noble path, right speech, attempting to rid my speech of barbaric language even when used for a good cause, for example, "warriors for peace," and endeavor to avoid denigrating speech;
- the realization that divine power works through every person, even though we tend to block it from having full effect;
- what Schweitzer called Reverence for Life as my guiding principle.

Virginia Ramey Mollenkott

VIRGINIA RAMEY MOLLENKOTT is professor emeritus at William Paterson University of New Jersey. She taught English language and literature for forty-four years and is the author of eleven books, including *The Divine Feminine* and *Sensuous Spirituality*.

In my peripheral vision there was a flash of greenish red, then a sickening thud against the windowpane. I jumped up from my desk, dreading what I would find—and, sure enough, on her side in the grass beneath my window lay a female cardinal. Nearby, her crimson partner stood his ground in anxious dignity.

The cat! I made a dive for the open door, lured the cat inside with the promise of treats, closed off her access to the out-of-doors. And then I waited. And waited. Hoped. And hoped. I knew these cardinals were recent parents. They had nested in a bush next to my bedroom window, and often they whistled me awake. Would this "royal lady" ever witness the flying of her young?

About an hour later, the one eye that I could see came open, staring at first but with a gradually, returning alertness. Good. Then she began to turn her head, cautiously righting herself. Later, a tentative hop. And finally, with great suddenness, she winged her way across the yard, low at first but then swinging upward.

What was it that stirred and lifted within me at her sudden return to glory? And what was it that did an inner dance later that day, when I saw her and her consort darting here and there across the front lawn, teaching their fledglings to fly?

How to name that sense of yearning connectedness, that interwoven web of oneness, that goddess-ground on which all being rests, that surging energy by which all things consist? I live and move within it, and it lives and moves within me, yet it is beyond my naming. Perhaps we might call it Love. Or Life.

To recognize and honor it is reverence.

To deny it is to delude oneself with the notion that differences like form, species, color, and function are ultimately important.

To deny connectedness is to deny reality. And that denial is merely a mistake, an illusion. Alas, however, in a world of diverse forms that certainly do appear to be separate and competing for scarce resources, the result of the illusion can be tragic. Inhumanity. Cruelty. Barbarism.

How then can we stimulate in one another the delicate fellow-feeling, the connected awareness, the reverence that deals not death but life? Here is our challenge, and it is a great one: to remind the human spirit that despite apparent differences, all of us have wings of one sort or another and are intended to fly.

Judith Thompson

JUDITH THOMPSON has worked with survivors of war and violence for twenty years. She founded and directed Children of War, an international youth leadership organization assisting young leaders from war zones to heal from trauma.

The work of Children of War is grounded in what I call four Cs: compassion, community, commitment, and courage. These are the things that are necessary for social transformation to happen on a broad scale.

Compassion implies an experience of connectedness to other human beings and the rest of creation. It must be at the center in order for any real change to take place. Compassion implies that the suffering of the world is my suffering. If I can feel the suffering of others and recognize their suffering is connected to my suffering, it can be the doorway to deep connectedness.

What amazes me is that some things are so basic but have been passed over time and again. Listening well and providing safe space is the most human thing in the world yet is so rarely done.

Learning how to be present to each other is the key to community. The merit of this work is offering opportunities for people to be present to each other in a way that is deeper and more authentic than they have ever been able to be. This is a life-generating thing.

This bonding has been particularly creative between U.S. inner-city youth and international war survivors. For young people in the inner city who have internalized a lot of negative self-concepts and who have limited experience of the world, getting connected to their peers from South Africa or Nicaragua helps them plug into a bigger experience of themselves. They, too, know war, they, too, have been oppressed by systemic racism and classism, they, too, are survivors, they, too, are strong and courageous, and they, too, can tell the truth about their pain, can weep for themselves and the world.

Commitment is a natural concomitant of compassion and community. Once the covenant is forged through sharing our lives and learning to listen and feel for, and with, each other, commitment to one another is the next step. When you become family with any group of people, you will naturally commit yourself to them, and if you don't there is usually an ideology about commitment. If all you're carrying with you is an ideology and not a relationship, a shared experience, you are more likely to feel burned out or compromise your beliefs.

The relationships have been absolutely sustaining for all of us involved. This kind of power interests me: both the power of individuals who, if you can assist them in their healing process, can move forward in their ability to do good things and the power inherent in relationship—in commitment to individuals, in commitment to each other, in commitment to the community. When we talk about what is the binding power of the universe, it's love— let's face it. People might use different words, but when you get down to it, love is an energy.

A lot of the work of Children of War was also to allow young people to retain, and many times to remember, the larger vision of the way the world could be to give them back their courage. Most people have this vision as children. At every opening talk I would put a big picture of the planet up and we would start to relate to that planet as home, as a living entity. We would start to talk about what we were like as children. What were our hopes? What did we believe in? What did we believe was possible? How big was our vision? People would say, "My vision was big—anything was possible." Then I would ask, "What do you believe now?" and the reply would be, "Well, not as much is possible." The work is helping people to reconnect with the vision that anything is possible.

The beauty of the work was we basically had experiential processes where people began to experience connectedness to each other, as well as a sense of self that was new and expanded. They were sharing that message through who they were being—and the radiance was palpable.

To be human? Traveling the road back home! People embody the world in themselves. When you can really be present with any individual you enter an entire universe. That's the beautiful mystery of the holographic universe—the whole is present in the parts. My intent is to find the world in individuals—to understand that love power, transformation power, change power that is released every time two individuals or fifty take the time to be present with one another.

Catherine de Vinck

Around each object
   a space of definition;
   around each face
   a diamond shield
   impossible to break.

And above all, a dazzling
     planetarium:
   stars in fusion, spinning moons
   rotating suns, a flaming display
   terrifying in its speed and power.

For an instant, yes, we are here
   beneath the spreaded branches
   of the tree of life
   a shelter of sorts
   under which voices continually speak
   weaving the web of language
   casting over the world
   a net of sounds.

CATHERINE DE VINCK is the author of eleven books of poetry that are nourished by ancient wisdom and grounded in empathy.

What are they saying that we ignore
    what messages do they bring
    what words to redeem and bless
    these times of resonant irony.

After we yank down
    the ragged drapes of history
    we enter a zone of disappearance
    the inner geography where chatter ends.
    In this vastness without borders
    in this archaic, sacred silence
    the original Face appears
    and the light turns and turns to us.

James Heisig

The Zen temple of Ryoan-ji in Kyoto, best known for its enigmatic fifteenth-century rock garden, houses another little treasure, unobtrusive as it is profound. Set among the greenery that runs along the outer porch is a small circular basin with a square font in the center used to draw water for the tea ceremony. The face of the stone is carved with four Chinese glyphs arranged in

JAMES HEISIG holds a doctorate from Cambridge University and has taught philosophy and religion in the United States and Latin America. He is currently the director of the Nanzan University Institute for Religion and Culture in Nagoya, Japan.

such a way that the square forms a part of each of them. Read clockwise they mean: *All I need to know is how much is enough.*

Day after day herds of tourists march by the basin without so much as a second thought. Meantime here we are at the end of the twentieth century, at last beginning to listen to the earth whose resources we have been devouring out of all control. It is also becoming ever more clear to us that global poverty and deprivation are not simply the result of cultural differences but are in fact required to sustain an upper crust of civilization for whose citizens surfeit is the measure of human fulfillment. But it has only just begun to dawn on us how empty that fulfillment really is. The more goods and services pile up, the shorter the span of enjoyment and the greater the demand for more of the same. This kind of mass asceticism masquerading as gluttony with a human face has in turn been advertised successfully as the ideal for the masses left behind in the march of progress.

All you need to know is how to be able to afford more.

The temple of Apollo at Delphi has an inscription carved in the wall of the cave which has become the cornerstone of philosophy ever since Socrates went there to consult the oracle: *gnothi sauton*— "know yourself." In homage to that simple injunction we have struggled for centuries to measure the depth of our humanness not in terms of education or possessions or rank but in terms of how far we know who we are and what kind of stuff we are made of. On the opposite wall is another, lesser known inscription: *me den agan*— "nothing in excess." It is time we balanced our long pursuit of knowing the self with a deliberate pursuit of knowing how much is enough—enough to enjoy to the full, enough to go around, enough to sustain the earth. The vocation is to a higher culture, had we only the ears to hear it.

Leonardo Lazarte

Reencountering the Human—What Are We Looking At?

LEONARDO LAZARTE is a professor of mathematics at the University of Brasília, Brazil. His interests include global issues and human development.

When still a child, I was impressed by an observation adults repeated rather regularly: Humans have conquered the atom, space, have produced marvelous technologies, but socially they have not advanced. I was intrigued by this statement. It seemed as if we had developed a great capacity for growth that was expressed in the conquests of science and technology but was not applied to social issues and relations between humans.

This statement was applied to expressions of human barbarism, a tacit condemnation of science and technology, and the reasoning that sustains them. Even though this perception seemed at times irrefutable, I was left to reflect why this was so—even if it really were so—why humans have not advanced in their fundamental attitudes, social relations, and ethics.

217

Even today this statement is not completely valid. Further reflection has shown me that our society has obtained exactly what it was looking for. We searched for domination of the world. We learned the scientific laws and applied them. Since we concentrated on the physical dimension, it is not surprising that our triumphs are found there.

Have we forgotten the human? In focusing on the material dimension our society has tried to understand everything else from this point of view. To recapture the integrity of the "human being" and Reverence for Life requires focusing our attention on the forgotten dimensions as well as on new dimensions. We are called to reencounter the spiritual dimension, to cultivate, with a new fervor, personal relationships, to discover how similar we are not only to our neighbors but also to people in every part of the world, and to feel vitally coresponsible for this great human monad.

What has been broken? Although Brazil is my adopted country, I spent the eighties in England. While there, I could not stop being concerned about Brazil's problems. It was precisely at this time that the urban violence, originally shown only in movies, transformed into a daily reality in the big cities such as Rio de Janeiro and São Paulo. From a distance, I pondered two questions: What happened to create such violence? What could be done to change this? I do not have any answers, but thinking about the problem has offered new insight about the nature of the disintegration of what it means to be human.

When I was an adolescent, I was confused sometimes about opposing ideologies and conflicting discourses. I had to learn about the concrete consequences they had for human lives. Speak about love and kill in its name? Kill elected presidents to defend democracy? Kill those who do not want to receive the "benefits" of the state? I was seeking less ideal conditions but ones which would not destroy the elements we consider fundamental: respect for human beings and Reverence for Life.

Today I am worried about increasing violence. For some time the political system imposed on Latin America required ignoring the needs and inhumane conditions of a large part of its people. This way of perceiving society, held by the elite in the society, became a basic attitude adopted by the entire society. When an elite group can ignore a mother whose children are dying from hunger, why wouldn't the poorest people incorporate a similar kind of behavior, learning to ignore the value of human life to steal a pair of imported shoes or other desired object for consumption?

There is an important detail. It is not misery that generates violence. It is the way society allows its members to be treated. Values of the diverse segments of society are increasingly interpenetrating, principally when they refer to such fundamental values as respect for the human condition.

What, then, is the human condition? Part of the human condition is to question what it is to be human. We raise this question when something has been broken in our society or in us—in moments of crisis. We question it when we want to discover where humanity is heading. We want to discover how to respond individually to the call of the matrix that contains us.

Today one of the principal foci of what it is to be human is not only individual identity but also reverence toward our fellow humans, related or distant. It has to do with autonomous individuals copenetrating with their local community and with the grand global monad for the well-being of all.

Rustum Roy

RUSTUM ROY is Evan Hugh Professor of the Solid State, professor of geochemistry, and professor of Science, Technology, and Society at Pennsylvania State University. He is a "radical pluralist," incorporating insights of science and technology into religion.

I believe in the whole of creation as the Reality, ground of Being, that I can experience—Good and Evil; Beauty and Ugliness; Truth and Falsehood.

———

I believe in the Absolute Transcendent Allness of Reality, the Absolute Wholeness of Existence. In the relative insignificance of the Universe out there (all the billions and billions of galaxies so far from me). In the relative, terrifying significance of all that is in here (all those billions and trillions of summer flowers in a meadow inviting all to run among them; all those billions and trillions of bacteria in every African well dealing sickness and death; all those

infinite trains coursing through every human mind of
thoughts, ideas, visions, the power of emotions,
arousal, and tranquillity; all the billions of my fellow
human beings who suffer more than they need to
because I and my kind do not care enough.

———

I believe in "God" the Father, who is also Mother,
Sister, Brother, as the name by which humans give
Reality a human face. Almighty, who is equally
utterly powerless, Maker of heaven and earth,
Creator who is also
the Creation of different
families of creatures.

———

I believe in Jesus Christ, love incarnate, window to
Enlightened One, and to all the Bodhisattvas:
Benedict, Francis, Hildegard, Rumi, Martin Luther,
and Martin Luther King, Archbishop Cranmer,
Dogen, Schweitzer, Mahatma Gandhi, Archbishop
Romero, and Dietrich Bonhoeffer, through whose lives
the light of Reality did shine, beacons on our Way.

———

I believe also in all the great prophets, Ikhnaton,
Zoroaster, Mohammed, Augustine and Thomas
Aquinas, the Father and Mother of the Iroquois and
the Sioux, the Ugro-Finnic shamans and countless
others who I know have been the windows for others,
my sisters and brothers throughout the world,
who believe as I do.

———

Rustum Roy   221

I believe utterly and operationally in the Holy
Spirit—the Essence which pervades all space and
time—which is the transcendent reality
accessible to me and to all, via quanta of
consciousness, when by word, thought and deed
I make that effort.

———————

I believe deeply and personally in the absolute
necessity of the Church, the atom, the indivisible particle
of human existence, the locus of collective
true being where two or three are gathered around
the same commitments. Only such a church can save
me from my irresponsible self, can serve my utterly
personal needs, can discipline me and
challenge me and succor me.

Tomin Harada

Looking back, it is hard to understand why Japan and China ever went to war, why I was inducted in my early twenties and hence constrained to be a participant in that war, which was expected to be over in a few months but instead became a global conflict. Once hostilities begin, reason is abandoned for animosity, revenge, and ever-escalating levels of hatred and cruelty.

TOMIN HARADA was a surgeon, born in Hiroshima. He helped to establish the first Japanese Reconstructive Medical Society and was the first chairman of the World Friendship Center, a meeting place for visitors to Hiroshima to learn firsthand about the horrors of nuclear war.

Sheer fanaticism ruled those years, until finally Japan, which had wreaked such violence, suffering, and death on millions of humans in other countries, saw almost a third of its own population killed and wounded. Farmers, merchants, teachers, doctors, people who had lived in peace for over three centuries, returned to Japan in rags, infested with lice, arms or legs missing, suffering from malnutrition. We were labeled criminals by the rest of the world, barred from international society. Many of us were ashamed of having survived the war at all.

Today, half a century later, the world is once more full of live coals that seem ready to burst into flame and we seem helpless to avoid such conflagrations.

Still, Hiroshima and Nagasaki stand as symbols of the unspeakable horror of modern nuclear war.

If this book on reverence versus contempt for life can reach the hearts of even a few people, there is still reason for hope, even for this octogenarian doctor who has witnessed the horrors, not only of the 200,000 fellow humans killed by nuclear violence and the many thousands of "delayed war deaths" from leukemia and other malignancies that followed in the decades since the Bomb was dropped.

On the cenotaph in Hiroshima's Peace Memorial Park these words are engraved: "Rest in Peace, for we shall not repeat this evil." It is not entirely clear who is promising not to repeat that evil. But it has often been suggested that the real meaning is: "All of humanity shall not repeat it," and with this I agree. We survivors never quite understood whether we were lucky or unlucky to have survived. Still, we should devote all our energies to seeing to it that this desecration of life will never happen again.

I saw Dr. Franck's drawing of Chio-san. On it he had written what she said, while she was posing.

> It used to be so simple, but now it is simple no longer. It is very painful to talk about it. For me it is as if it happened yesterday, those people, those thousands shuffling in total silence like a line of ants through the devastation . . .
>
> I am an old woman now, almost ninety. Who listens to me? But we Japanese should be workers for peace constantly, but we ignore our task. We have become all too

obsessed with money instead of with the Mystery of Being Alive.

Confucius would have spoken of compassion, the Buddha of mercy, the Christ of love for one's neighbor. Albert Schweitzer called it Reverence for Life.

Annelie Keil

ANNELIE KEIL is a professor of sociology, health, and education at the University of Bremen, Germany, where she is a television host and commentator working on themes and topics related to health and human change.

There is no true source of wisdom except life itself. There is no greater need than to learn from it and journey with it now, when we are submerged in a kind of worldwide darkness, full of false gods, insensitive ideologies, and rampant inhumanity to humans and nature. Yet the fundamentally human is imperishably ever-present, as I discovered living my own life in the midst of twentieth-century barbarism.

I was born at the beginning of the Second World War and my first experience of life was abandonment. I was placed in an orphanage in Poland, because I was an "unfortunate accident" of an uncaring and nonloving relationship. Dependent and helpless, I had to accept what life taught me in those first days after birth: There is no certainty or even promise of anything. I did not choose my parents; I didn't choose the year of war for my birth. I just fell into earth, a little homeless star looking for a landing place. And there I was. The nurses in the orphanage did their best to be mothers and we little ones tried to get what we needed: a hug, a smile, someone to play with, someone to feed us. Abandonment does not mean that there is nobody around.

We receive the gift of life as a possibility. Only in the process of being do we get to know what our life is about and how we can develop into human beings even in these barbaric times.

What I experienced as a child seemed to be something like the essence of life. Our biographies are a lifelong attempt to integrate the universal aspects of life with our own experiences in concrete situations, many of which we don't like, many of which make us suffer.

As an abandoned child, I sensed my potential of being alive, had no doubt that my having been born had its reason. I felt that there was meaning to it all, and I started out discovering it. Children are very serious in questioning the world's realities; that is why they are so busy with themselves. They are facing the "why" and the "why not."

By walking, hearing, smelling, moving, thinking, feeling, and touching, in our own way we develop and unfold life by learning to use our senses, our bodies, our minds, our social relations, our spirituality.

In 1945 my mother took me out of the orphanage. Apparently it was easier for her to flee the Russians with a child. Still, on my sixth birthday, we ended up in a Russian prison camp. Once, trying to steal food in that camp, I was caught by a Russian officer. Looking into my frightened eyes, he recognized the longing and anxiety of his own little daughter, who together with her family was killed near Leningrad by the Germans. He started crying and as he smiled at me through his tears, we joined hands. Two homeless people, without any words, decided to take care of each other, to be father and daughter. This lasted for nearly two years—the only time in my life that I ever had a father.

This experience deepened my understanding of human life. I learned that life in its fullest sense exists only when the appropriate conditions for living are provided. There is neither individual nor social life, unless we create it. This I knew before thinking about it and becoming politically engaged.

Humankind has a natural responsibility for the continuity of its life; thus a decision must be constantly made to make life possible.

After the war, in my daily attempts to survive, I could feel the rhythmic dance of life between becoming and passing away. I felt that the dance could fail at any moment, that life unfolds in the face of risks and resistance. Light needs shadow to exist. As a Native American proverb says: "The soul would have no rainbow if the eyes had no tears."

If we dare not face our fears we forever have to run from them. Recommendations like "don't take risks," "don't experiment," "just stay," "trust the experts," are the most dangerous ones for both social and democratic life and for personal health in the deepest sense.

As a child I was more open to the wisdom of life than later on, when I had been trained, hence somehow spoiled, as a scientist. Life is bound by a paradigm of self-organization, reaching beyond our limitations, and true reality.

We are not "holistic" by ourselves! Holism can only be a daily practice, an active "self-integration," as Hans Jonas says, a task that can fail or succeed. We are homeless and find truth and a home by living life unconsciously. I learned to follow the essential principle of life, after which I started to fight for social and human rights consciously. Even though this was important, my own spiritual path became much more complicated. Getting politically involved in achieving goals, I often lost trust in my life experiences. The roots of love, exchange, cooperation, connectedness, responsibility, compassion, movement, transformation of birth and death are indispensable ingredients of our physical and spiritual life. They are part of a biology of hope and love that helps to relate to these sources when we are aware of them and dare to make decisions.

Life is not a program. It seems to be an invitation, a challenge to take the next step into the darkness of uncertainty and creativity. In pursuing models and ideologies rather than life itself, looking for safety, trying to insure oneself against risks, one walks into a trap, for there is no life insurance coverage we can buy. No one else can live our lives!

But how can we bear the suffering that comes out of this uncertainty and openness? I had to give up my adopted father when we were sent home to freedom in Germany after the war. After years of being a prisoner, I did not feel at home or free at all. I was homeless again because I had lost the only one who really took care of me. There was nothing to live for in this freedom.

In West Germany I learned what it means to be a refugee, to be poor and dependent on social welfare, to have no family, to be unwelcome. I was not programmed by any religious belief system. My mother said that religion was a drug for stupid people. Still I recognized in my own child's way that "faith is the feeling of life in oneself" (Wilhelm Reich). And I learned that the capacity to believe has been bestowed upon us as a primeval function and necessity to survive. It is a source of hope, a solidarity of living things. In the midst of desperation, hunger, and discrimination, there is always a little help from friends. Only if we value being part of the universal order can we see the hunger of another being as our own. If we see someone who is homeless or ill, it is an invitation to create life, and to help now!

This prime religious drive that makes sense we share as a necessity of the soul. It cannot be surrendered or be violated without serious injury to the individual and to the societies in which we live.

Feeling abandoned after a profound love relationship, as an adult woman I developed cancer. I had to lose something very important to be able to create life anew. Illness may be needed to understand health as a holistic and deep approach to life, instead of as punishment for something done wrong. Sickness is not something ascribable to illness-generating risk factors. Illness and health are in an interplay like darkness and light. Looking back to the experiences of my childhood and reflecting on them, I can better face up to my own problems and the problems of the society in which I live.

Becoming more and more imprisoned behind the walls of separation and competition, our society is losing the human language of sharing and of communality. The gap between rich and poor, between nations, between races is increasing. Dizzied by our capacity to destroy, we have moved away from reality and have come to believe in a "virtual reality" produced for the purpose of making money.

We are living in a century of arrogant stupidity. An ancient wisdom has been replaced by intellectual narcissism and extreme ignorance. Our true source of wisdom is life itself, and in the imperishably ever-present and specifically human there is hope.

Arthur Frank

Too many creeds have given credo writing a bad name: Political, religious, and economic belief systems seem to have elevated humanity less often than they have provided rationales for oppression and conflict. But when the world has had enough institutional creeds, perhaps we need more

ARTHUR FRANK is a professor in the department of sociology at the University of Calgary. He is the author of *At the Will of the Body: Reflections on Illness* and *The Wounded Storyteller: Body Illness and Ethics.*

personal credos. Is it now possible, at this moment of the historical exhaustion of belief systems, to write one's personal credo in the hope of affecting others but emphatically not of converting them? Can I invite you to entertain certain of my beliefs, as one entertains a guest? I ask for the hospitality of an honestly open ear and offer assurance that I will not overstay my welcome.

I believe in stories more than in principles, so I begin with the story of a credo that has lingered in my ear for over thirty years. In my first year at university I took a course in European literature. At the end of his last lecture the professor allowed himself to offer us some advice. He repeated an aphorism by Goethe that his father had told him: "Every day one should read a poem, look at a work of art, and listen to some music." I've carried that aphorism with me as an aesthetic credo that the mundane deserves to be informed by the artistic. But for now I am less interested in what Goethe said than in why I was so receptive to my professor's quotation.

The best account I can give of my receptivity is that I felt the professor had earned the right to give us such advice and we had earned the right to receive it. Both professor and students had worked hard that semester, reading, writing, and talking about books that stretched us to imagine different worlds viewed in different ways. On both sides, the professor's and ours, Goethe's aesthetic credo had been hard won; we had earned the right to such words.

Thus, before all else, I believe that credos must be hard won. Books of quotations are full of fine aphorisms, but when aphorisms are read in such books—which delete the work of having gotten to those words—their effect on the reader can be aesthetic in the ephemeral sense of merely pleasing.

Thus I believe a credo is a statement not of principles but of process. This process is one of perpetual reflection on how we live our lives, with the purpose of understanding how our choices have made us who we are and the end of choosing more wisely, informed by a vision of who we might become.

A credo is a life's foundation, and my foundation lies in shifting ground. My work is to teach students who are less disillusioned than they are simply untouched by visions of the ideal. Those who place their beliefs in institutional religions are too often unthinking, and those whose institutional experiences have left them willing to speak only of personal spirituality lack discipline. At the moment when their lives should be an unfolding project, the work they are able to imagine as available holds little prospect of careers in the sense of personal development through work. I see people of all ages whose conception of politics lacks any vision of community and society, having been reduced to the personal gain of a tax benefit and the resentment satisfied by the layoff of some government employees. I constantly listen to people whose sense of relation to others is based in opposition. Two men are discussing health care: "We cannot afford it," one says, referring to government expenditures for care. The "it" might be a shorter waiting list for surgery or emergency room care, or "it" might be a new school or a job-training program. My ear is caught less by "it" than by his use of "we." His "we" seems to comprise persons who have no stake in the lives of most other persons. This man does not say, "Our health care system [or education or corporations] must become differently tuned, in order to be more sensitive to diverse needs of a diverse population." He divides the world into "we" who pay and "they" who receive. Secure on his side of a divide that his thinking has constructed as unbroachable, he measures out his political will in resentment. I wonder when a heart attack or cancer will drag him across that divide, out of the security of his "we" into the maelstrom of those who are unaffordable.

Where do I start from, that I see and hear these things as I do? Ten years ago I was dragged, not gently but in supreme stillness, across my own divide. I had an aberrant heart attack, caused by a virus. I crossed a divide but did not recognize the crossing. I understood the import of what had happened as little more than medical. Less than a year after being discharged from cardiac care I was diagnosed with cancer. In the years following my own surgery and treatment I watched relatives and friends die and I learned that the medical aspects of what happened to us were the very least of the drama, a necessary least, but not what the divide we crossed was about. What counted was the communion of mortality.

I believe in the supreme value of knowing we are going to die because only this knowledge, thrown back in my face over and over, has been capable of changing me in ways that I am thankful for. Only suffering, with its certain intimation of death, can reform my sense of who I am and cause me to reimagine that most important question: What is my stake in the lives of others?

I call my credo the pedagogy of suffering, a phrase that recollects my profession of teaching and my history of illness and that offers a tribute to what it takes to make me rethink who I am in relation to others. Only in suffering has the boundary of my sense of "we" loosened; only in suffering do I reach across that invisible divide and touch others, not to impress them or to gain their adherence but to reassure us both that in our suffering we are not alone.

The pedagogy of suffering teaches me that the only beginning is at the weakest point and what begins is a story. During the last decade my own beginning has often been the biblical story of Jacob, in whom I see myself most clearly. The young Jacob believes in his tricks, and if he himself is tricked in return, the question is how his own proclivity for trickery has rendered him liable. At his weakest moment, after he has stolen his father-in-law's household gods and as his brother's forces are poised to attack him, he dreams of wrestling with an other whom he does not know. In this wrestling he realizes that the other who can wound him also can bless him. With a new name, he begins a new story, which is also a retelling of all that has gone before; his past is not forgotten, but it can be given a different necessity.

The pedagogy of my own sufferings gives new necessity to what I know but practiced inadequately because my knowledge is insufficiently hard won. The only words I can put to this knowledge do no more than designate values most of us share: *craftsmanship, focus, proportion,* and more complex still, *self-reflection* and *responsibility.* The great word encompassing all these may be *love,* but perhaps *love* has become too big a word; the pedagogy of suffering teaches me to think small, or at least as small as the extent of my sufferings has as yet allowed me to think. The pedagogy of suffering teaches that we do not need many beliefs, just enough to direct our work, to sustain us in sorrow, and to provide for gratitude.

The beliefs that have been hardest won for me might be called negative, since the pedagogy of suffering teaches through negation. Suffering requires discovering what fills experiences that society often construes as emptying.

I believe in being caught off guard. In certain moments I have the privilege of seeing a stranger and then realizing that he is I. These moments remind me I am less the image I prepare to see as myself; rather, I am someone with a greater share of all the faults I see in others. But being caught off guard is also central to the capacity to create. I believe I can prepare for acts of creating and I can intentionally refine what has been created, but the moment of creation must catch me off guard. This moment is pure grace, and gratitude is the true response.

I believe in interruption. I set out to write this credo. First I was interrupted by the troubles of a friend who is separating from her husband and worries for their child; then I was interrupted by the need to care for children of family members going to a funeral; then I was called to visit a stranger who is hospitalized with cancer; finally, and most pleasantly, my daughter burst into my study, wanting me to affirm her joy at being who she is on another day. I realize that these are not interruptions in my credo; they are what I believe. Their shifting and conflicting demands are my center. My beliefs are nothing more than my responses to these other persons, with their joys and troubles.

I believe in insecurity and vulnerability. In my cynical moments I believe in the new viruses capable of initiating an epoch of plagues that some scientists think may reduce the world's population by a third. Perhaps such a culling is the only remedy for our decadence. Wars and their holocausts have not taught us; if anything, the rebuilding in their aftermath seems to have fed humanity's hubris. If I myself have changed for the better only in moments when my own patent vulnerability has effaced any boundary of security I once drew around myself, perhaps society needs the democracy of some airborne plague to teach us common cause. As a society we believe too much in our own tricks; we minimize our wounds rather than seek blessing in them.

The pedagogy of suffering may build on shifting ground, but it teaches that even though the ground is shifting, the center can still hold. As a center, suffering is both what we shared in common with one another and what is ours uniquely. Suffering teaches the distinctiveness in the universal: If mortality is our point of communion, the roads to our individual deaths are like snowflakes. Each unique and consummately beautiful form exists only for its own moment of drift.

I would not presume to think that snowflakes can neither appreciate their beauty nor direct their flights; I know only that people surely can do both. Our lives are what we craft, and that crafting is our responsibility.

To live is to write one's credo, every day in every act. I pray for a world that offers us each the gift of reflective space, the Sabbath quiet, to recollect the fragments of our days and acts. In those recollections we may see a little of how our lives affect others and then imagine, in the days ahead, how we might do small and specific acts that create a world we believe every person has a right to deserve.

Thomas Bezanson

Years ago, when I became committed to the art of pottery, I had a vision of the "perfect pot."

It haunted my imagination, even my dreams.

It was an utterly "simple" form; it had a beautiful shining white glaze. The whole thing was so consummately beautiful that it was almost not there. A fragile, vulnerable, unearthly beauty.

In my youthful ignorance and in my "tiger years," I poured my energies into concretizing that vision. They were the years of a thousand failures. Of course, I never achieved that perfect pot or even came close to it.

The vision faded and so did my zeal for it. Then one day, twenty-five years later, the vision came back while I was in Japan. It was a brand-new vision: That pot was myself. I realized that if I ever were to make that sublimely beautiful pot I must first become that sublimely beautiful person. The artist and the person saw that the

THOMAS BEZANSON is a ceramic artist and a Benedictine monk. His work is in museum collections in North America, Europe, and Japan.

beauty of the spider's web comes out of the beauty of the spider's being.

As an ancient Sufi saying has it: "Some doors open only from the inside."

Anne Wilson Schaef

When I was four years old, we lived in Fayetteville, Arkansas. The year was 1938. We lived there from 1938 until 1941. Like many others at that time, we did not have much money. Yet I remember those years as being good ones. My mother was a passionate woman, and the older I get the more and more grateful I am for the early lessons she taught me—usually not just in words.

ANNE WILSON SCHAEF is an internationally known writer, lecturer, organizational consultant, philosopher, and workshop leader. Her books include *Meditations for Women Who Do Too Much* and *Living in Process*.

We lived only a few blocks from "the square" in the center of town, and Mother and I often walked uptown to do our shopping. Often we would see a young retarded man selling pencils on the street corner, and in spite of our meager financial resources, Mother always managed to put something in his tin cup. One day, when we rounded the corner, we encountered a group of teenagers teasing the man, spilling his pencils all over the street. My mother swung into action. She was about five feet tall—and very slim. Before my eyes, she grew to what looked to me (and I am sure those big boys!)

239

to be about eight feet tall! She grabbed a couple of them by the nape of the neck or an ear and in no uncertain terms told them that she was appalled with their behavior . . . had they no upbringing? She insisted that they pick up the man's pencils and return them to him, apologize, and pay him for anything damaged—which they did with great deference to her.

She then made her ususal deposit in his cup and we went on about our business.

All human beings are precious and those of us with gifts have a responsibility to those less fortunate and weaker to see that they are respected and protected.

One lovely spring day, my four-year-old eyes spotted the beautiful spring flowers in the garden of a big house down the street from where we lived. I decided that they would make a lovely gift for my mother and I "picked" some, roots and all! When I presented them to her, she asked where I had found them. I took her to the house and lovely garden where they had been growing. All the way down the street, Mother talked to me about the flowers not being mine, how sad it was to pull up such beautiful growing things, however much she appreciated my wanting to give her a gift. We went to the front door, knocked, and waited. An ancient (or so she looked to me) black woman came to the door. I remember seeing, but not understanding, the uneasiness in her eyes as she saw a young white mother and child on her doorstep. Mother introduced us and told her that I had come to apologize for pulling up her flowers. She immediately assumed the deferent downcast eyes and manner of a black woman in the 1930s in Arkansas, said her name was Adelaide, and excused my behavior—"Don't you give it no mind. She don't mean no harm. That's all right. She's just little." "No, it isn't all right," said Mother. "Elizabeth Anne, you tell 'Miss Adelaide' that you are sorry. Give her back her flowers and tell her you will help her replant them if she wishes." (In the South we were always taught to call older maiden ladies and widows Miss in those days. However, few granted that respect to blacks!) In replanting the flowers, "Miss Adelaide" and I became good friends.

We are all one human family. All members are worthy of respect. We should never trod over others or their property just because we can. We are responsible for our behavior and our actions no matter how young we are or how innocent the motive. It is our responsibility to see how our actions affect others and to do what we can to right a wrong we have created.

We are part of a larger whole. There is a mystery greater than ourselves, and all of creation experiences the unconditional love of that mystery and participates in it. When we destroy or damage any part of God's creation, we abuse and destroy ourselves. Being fully human means accepting the responsibility of knowledge that we are one with all things. We have no choice. These responsibilities are our birthright.

At sixty-two, these lessons are as clear to me as they were when I was four and I see how they have guided and informed my life. In my mother I was gifted with a great teacher.

Ervin Laszlo

ERVIN LASZLO is founder and president of the Club of Budapest. He is a leading exponent of systems and is the author of sixty-two books.

In the closing years of the twentieth century humankind has reached a crucial juncture: the threshold of a new stage not merely of economic and technological but also of social and spiritual evolution. Societies are evolving out of the nationally based industrial systems created at the dawn of the first industrial revolution and heading toward an interconnected, information-based system that straddles the globe.

The critical juncture we have reached is not unprecedented insofar as it augurs a fundamental change, but it is unprecedented inasmuch as it indicates a change of planetary dimensions. Human societies have changed all along their long and eventful history: They are complex systems that maintain themselves in an environment that is itself changing. But change hitherto was mainly local, and it could be dealt with by local action. And if such action failed, societies could always settle or conquer fresh territories and tap fresh supplies of natural resources. Today, however, humanity has become a global species, operating on the edge of the sustainability of its planetary abode. It is damaging, and in part destroying, essential aspects of that abode.

The processes in nature that ensure a sustainable environment have long delay times—changes we introduce today will have their effect years, perhaps decades, from now. But unless we introduce these changes now, the planet will become, if not entirely unlivable, at least incapable of supporting the over 6 billion people that will soon populate the six continents.

Can we make such necessary changes in time? One thing is clear: Continuing to produce facts and figures, numbers and statistics, will not be enough. People will shrug them off, saying that it is not their responsibility or that they alone cannot do anything about them. If this blindness and irresponsibility continues for just a few more years, it will be too late to do anything meaningful about the human condition. Millions, if not billions, of people will be condemned to starvation and disease, jobless and helpless in an unlivable environment. Violence is likely to erupt, and the enormous arsenals of weapons in the hands of governments—and, increasingly, in those of terrorists—may be put to terrible use, and the days of our species could be numbered.

Are we rushing blindly and helplessly toward our demise? Perhaps not. There must be deeper forces and higher powers we can appeal to. Could it be a matter of indifference to the forces and powers that brought about the human species on this planet, its spirit, its consciousness, this spirit and consciousness now threatened with final extinction? It is an urgent wake-up call, a call to the full realization of the sacredness of life.

For several years now, responsible public-spirited people and organizations have issued forecasts and warnings, exhortations and policy suggestions. Their effect has been too small and too slow. In recent years I have become increasingly convinced that we must try another approach: a recourse to the power of the spirit and the creativity of art. These powers must help us to evolve a new consciousness, give birth to a new sense of responsibility, to a new ethos and a new ethics. It is our last resource. It may, however, be a real and powerful resource. We do not know just how real and how powerful until we begin to develop it.

These are insights and thoughts that have led me to found the Club of Budapest, an organization dedicated to the proposition that if we are to turn around the current doomsday trend, we must appeal to the deepest insights and highest powers of humanity. We must enlist the insights of the world's advanced spiritual persons. With their help and guidance we could have a chance to create the basis for a new planetary consciousness capable of measuring up to the threats and the problems and able to meet the challenges of a time that is soon running out.

The hour is late but, perhaps, not too late. Enlisting the powers of the spirit in the great venture of ensuring a future for humanity must begin. With the creation of initiatives such as the A-B C and the Club of Budapest, and an alliance among them, a new era could dawn of nonbarbaric civilization guided by the power of the spiritual forces resident in our endangered but not ultimately extinction-bound species.

James Earl Jones

To me humanness implies harmony and mutual caring among us humans.

"Inhumanity" is unnatural; it goes against our intrinsic human nature. Conflict, too, is natural, but conflicts can be solved without resorting to cruelty, without denying our humanness. We tend to define this humanness by contrasting it to its opposite, yet our humanness will express itself unless blocked by mean-spiritedness, by degrees of insanity, certified or not, or by plain evil.

JAMES EARL JONES is an African-American actor whose work in theater, on television, and in films has led him to be one of the most recognizable voices in the landscape of the American mass media.

We don't have to worry that in celebrating and praising the human in us we demean or diminish the awe of the Divine, of God.

As to myself, I hold that life is so valuable that even if I were the sole human being on the planet, life would still be meaningful and a joy. To share it, however, to be in the company of my fellow human beings, is sheer bliss, pure blessedness.

Mel King

MEL KING is a community organizer, political activist, author, and teacher in Boston, Massachusetts. He is currently involved in educational and cultural projects that focus on access to new technologies in inner-city communities.

What it means to be human. When I think about what it really means to be human many images come into view. One image that makes me really aware is what happens when a rock or pebble is thrown into the water, creating ripples that go on and on. What it means to be human is to be impacted by the ripples that are coming from people everywhere.

Being human means knowing that I am both at the center and on the edge of those ripples, that I have the capacity to impact and be impacted by others in many ways.

Being human for me recognizes that there is a symmetry and harmony in those ripples, that when the ripples that are coming from many directions envelop and join in the ripples that come from me we create a field of energy: the energy that is the source of our spirituality, without which none can survive, grow, or develop to one's infinite potential.

Being human, for me, then, is being in harmony with the gifts of creation. Being human is seeing yourself in others. Being human is understanding that we are gifts of creation and that in turn we have the gift to create.

Being human is understanding the art of me, the art of we. Being human is being able to express love for all: to feel, to think, to wonder, to be in awe of the majesty of it all.

Being human is being able to smile, to sing, to feel, to bring out the gifts of creation, to think out loud, to feel inside, to be in love and know that we can be loving.

Ralph White

RALPH WHITE is cofounder and director of the New York Open Center. He is also editor of *Lapis Magazine*.

I am deeply convinced that each one of us is an essentially spiritual being and that we contain within ourselves potentials of great creativity and beauty. We are, however, living in a materialistic civilization, and hence it is our task to reawaken in it an awareness of the good, the true, and the beautiful by initiatives that reflect attachment to these perennial values, catalysts to what is truly human in our world.

For as humans we live in conditions of profound interrelatedness with one another and with nature. I see it therefore as our responsibility to all fellow humans but also to animals and plants and to future generations to create an environment which acknowledges and takes account of our interdependence and our mutuality also with other life-forms. Living in a multiethnic, multicultural world with its innumerable traditions, I believe that we have the opportunity of fostering a planetary culture in which the spiritual and cultural treasures of all peoples can be honored and we can be enriched by the wisdom of all spiritual traditions, both individually and collectively. There exists a dark shadow in our psyche—individual as well as collective—that hides everything that we are unable to accept in ourselves both as persons and as collectives. We have no choice now but to summon the courage to face this shadow as honestly and persistently as we can, for unless we do we are bound to project on others what we dare not face in ourselves, with disastrous consequences. History is littered with too many holocausts to be ignored.

Tolerance and openness are indispensable for coexistence on this small planet. They are adequately expressed in the Universal Declaration of Human Rights. These principles together with a commitment to sustainable economic structures and harmony with the environment point toward a sane human future.

However, the increasing influence of a soulless, dehumanizing technology which intrudes unceasingly into every private life, a technology allied with the exclusive pursuit of profit, presents a formidable threat to such a sane future. Unless we humanize the machines and use them creatively we become machines in service to a mechanical idol. Technology, which "makes life easier" for many people, is not an end in itself. It exists for humans but not the other way around. So is economics developed to serve humans and not the other way around, to serve economic theories based on self-interest as the only consistent, predictable motivation.

Nevertheless I believe firmly that we humans frequently act out of altruistic impulses and compassion. Our models of technological and economic development must recognize it. I believe equally that human beings are propelled by the wish for freedom in its many forms with greater vigor than any other desire save that for love itself. A society stands judged by the degree to which it encourages and commits its members to develop within themselves the capacity for love and freedom. Economic, technological, and educational structures must serve these goals, for human life is sacred and each life cut short by either a person or the state brutalizes our awareness of that sacredness. Vengeance should not be encoded in legal statutes in a civilized society. I have no doubt that we must resist the seductions of an ever more superficial and materialistic mass culture, the ravages of profit-driven television and advertising, if we are to preserve contact with the inner self, with the truly human. Only by accepting and affirming ourselves in our deepest recesses and developing educational means that cultivate this sensitivity can we unfold our creative gifts, become fully human instead of pale, robotlike caricatures of our true potential, and create a society based on human rights, justice, ecological realities, and the alleviation of suffering which the times ahead of us demand.

Ramón Pascuel Muñoz Soler

A fundamental transformation is taking place at the end of this century. The world has become unrecognizable.

The biological clock is striking a new hour. What is happening? We travel through outer space but wonder about our children. At school we are programmed to give science

RAMÓN PASCUEL MUÑOZ SOLER is an Argentine physician, author, and lecturer who has written five books on synthesis and human futures. Written in Spanish, his work has been translated into English, German, and Portuguese.

and technology the last word, but in the maelstrom of our civilization we long to hear the first word.

I spent my childhood in a little provincial town, playing with children my age, making my toys, singing songs in the kitchen together with my parents, my sisters, reading Jules Verne. When I was fifteen I wrote a little book, *Greatness of Soul*, of which I still have the manuscript. I entrusted the secret of my heart to it. I did not lack anything. Yet at times I was assailed by a strange sadness. I wanted to know. I looked at the starry skies, I prayed to the Unknown, to God. There was no answer.

It was a first shudder of cosmic exile. From an early age I wanted to know, to understand, but since neither God nor the starry skies provided the answer, I began to be preoccupied with what it was to be a human being. So, instead of the heavens, I journeyed the highways of science, philosophy, literature, and history.

They, too, refused to answer my questions. I no longer searched for the essence of being human; I became aware of human needs, of human sorrow. So I chose to study medicine and became acquainted with disease, with old age and birth and death, with anguish, despair, insanity. It was an existential confrontation, because I arrived at a barrier hard to cross which could be called the crust of the human phenomenon, while the sense of my own being eluded me. As I examined and explored more deeply the meaning of life, I stumbled on my own shadow. It was a providential encounter; it was an inner voice that told me as it told Dante: *A te convien un altro viaggio.*

My travel was along the invisible path of the soul. I rediscovered that the human I had been looking for "outside," hidden by the veils of sorrow, disease, and death, was "inside" as well. In order to unveil the meaning of existence the light of intellect did not suffice; it required the transmutation of my own matter into light.

All those patterns of humanism I had searched, the humanism of the Renaissance, of socialism, of spiritualism, collapsed. I confronted my own destiny alone. Marx, who spoke of philosophers who had speculated about the world, assured us that "we have come to transform it." But this assertion took on another meaning: In my journey back to myself, I had come to transform myself! I had learned that the humanization and socialization of the world was not accomplished through the opposites of dialectics but by the reversal of values.

For twenty years I did not lecture, did not attend meetings, did not write any books, until at the end of this self-imposed abstinence I felt the need to transmit to others my spiritual experiences. And so in 1966 I wrote in Spanish *Germs of the Human Future*, and I also wrote five other books attempting to symbolically bridge the gap between the path of knowing, of science, and that of life.

How to interpret the end of the century, so laden with signs of hope and barbarism? I think we have gone too far. We are proceeding at high speed in the wrong direction. We are mistaken in our notion of time: The time of politics, economy, society, technology, and even the rhythm of our own life is not human time.

Something essential has escaped us.

Even as late as 1968 there was still some hope of re-creating the earth and life on earth. But today the time is gone; the words are exhausted; philosophical speculations about the world have become obsolete; the ones who promised transformation have vanished. Instead the goddess of technology has brought her message of salvation. The time of sacrifice has come as it always does on the threshold of new civilizations. We have crossed a perilous frontier. Not only is cybernetic time not human time, but our human functions have been marginalized, estranged from cosmic time, cosmic life. Work has become an adjustable variable for the schedules of economy; sex has been exchanged for love; our houses have become transitory shelters.

It is not a time for the soul's illumination but of the sacralization of matter. It is no longer a question of winning the world or saving the soul. It is a question of metanoia, of reconstructing the Temple.

I don't believe in academia, congresses, symposia, declarations of principle. I believe in work, sacrifice, and above all renunciation of the superfluous. I believe in the testimony of the protagonists of a new world, a new history, and in the shared inspiration of sages and saints to redesign, re-create a new integrated science of humanness for a civilization at the point of being born. Albert Schweitzer is one of the foremost of these protagonists. He is not a figure of the past but an announcer of the future if our species is to have a future.

TO BE HUMAN is to recognize the cultural perspectives that bind us to tribe, sect, religion, or nation and to rise above them. It is to feel the pain of the dispossessed, the downtrodden, the refugees, the slaves, the starving child.

Daniel Berrigan

The Law, The Poet (a poet released from prison, under condition that he apologizes for
his poetry.)

The poet recanted
they hacked off his fingers
and gave him a signet ring.

The poet recanted
they tore out his tongue
and crowned him their laureate.

He was then required
to flay himself alive.
Two houses of congress
applauded, they dressed him
in the Aztec cloak of immortals

The poet surrendered his soul
a bird of paradise

DANIEL BERRIGAN and his
brother Philip, along with Thomas
Merton and Thich Nhat Hanh,
were leaders in the religious
opposition to the Vietnam War. He
lives in New York City and
continues to work as a peace
activist. His latest book is *Isaiah*.

on a tray of silver held
in his two hands.
His soul flew away
the poet
by prior instruction
vanished where he stood.

Denizé Lauture

Answer
Are you present?
Absent?
Alive?
Dead?
Weeping in solitude?
Drill a hole
Into the thinking skull
And hook up
Your electrode
On the chart
The love's line
Will not vacillate
From the coordinates zero
Love is dead
But buried regretfully
Like the hatchet
Of a warmonger

DENIZÉ LAUTURE is a Haitian poet who has published several books of poems in English, French, and Creole.

Wilma Mankiller

WILMA MANKILLER was chief of the Cherokee Nation for over ten years. She was awarded the Presidential Medal of Freedom in 1998.

To be human is to understand our own insignificance in the totality of things. We are interdependent with plants, animals, water, the stars, the moon, the sun, to sustain our lives. Each has its own purpose and unique place in the universe.

To be human is to be concerned about spirituality, whether one expresses it through an orthodox religion, ancient ceremonies, or simply by the way we live our lives. Spiritual people ask, "How can I live my life in a good way?"

Christians may describe that quest as trying to be Christlike while a traditional Iroquoian might describe it as having a good mind. My favorite Cherokee prayer begins, "First let us remove all negative thoughts from our mind so we can come together as one. . . ." It is believed that even negative thoughts can permeate one's being and bring about negative actions.

To be human means to demonstrate love in the deepest, most

radical way, whether for a strong moon, powerful mountain, or another human being. Some people hoard love as if it would dissipate when shared with people or things outside their individual romantic interest or their own socially constructed nuclear family.

In historical times, our people, the Cherokee, referred to themselves as Real People. If Real People means being linked to everything and everyone around us, we remain the Real People. Some traditional Cherokee people continue to speak in our language about the gift of medicine from plants, the friendship of the wind, or ceremonies around the sacred fire. People who are not Cherokee in the larger society around us talk on cell phones about mutual funds, the right schools for their children, and always and forever, their weight and looks. Which seems more real? Which seems more human?

Catherine Bernier

CATHERINE BERNIER has been a teacher and administrator in the field of special education in North America. She served in the Peace Corps in Sri Lanka and lives in Colorado.

Up with the rising sun on a wheat-dried summer day, a man eats bowls of rancid rice. Green tea seeps through his soul. He walks down the street in flip-flop sandals perhaps to the river stalls, perhaps to buy fish. In his mind wander halibut or hailstones or the seeds of a small poem. In an instant all the greens of the earth, the blues of water and the skies, the reds and browns of flowing blood become the purest white, the white of all colors under the sun, the flash of a monstrous dawn.

Mushroom cloud
Grows from age to age
Splitting souls

The winds of all worlds press into a mythic fist, smash against the insect man, wedding him to seared cement. Balls of rain with fission flakes pelt his flattened form. When all that's left is smoke and fog and the fading cries of a loon, his wife, her skin in shreds, looks for him. She passes by the walking shadow pressed forever on the street, God's chop on the millennium.

Torn atoms
Nuclear rain falling
Still human

Constance Carlough

CONSTANCE CARLOUGH was a high school teacher in Fair Lawn, New Jersey, and is currently a therapist and addiction counselor in Middletown, New York.

When I am human I trace the filigree of the leaf with my eyes, I brush the tips of the leaf with my fingers, I hear the whir of the fly in my solar plexus, I become indistinguishable from other life.

Alas, how infrequently I am human!
I know, more than I believe, the dignity at the core of all life and
    celebrate that life whether it is seen through the spangle of a
    filament of spider's web,
        the tip of the trunk of a behemoth, the beleaguered feather of a
    factory chicken, or the eyelash of a despot.
When I see the raw cruelty of life I try to refrain from inflicting
    pain, but at the same time not
        rescuing life from necessary suffering.
I am silent in the face of the singing of life,
    in the awe of its being!

David Krieger

To be human is to break the ties of cultural conformity and group-think and to use one's own mind. It is to recognize good and evil and to choose good. It is to consider with the heart. It is to act with conscience.

DAVID KRIEGER is founder and president of the Nuclear Age Peace Foundation.

To be human is to be courageous. It is to choose the path of compassion, rather than the path of complacency. It is to break the silence and be an unrelenting advocate of human decency and human dignity. It is to sacrifice for what is just.

To be human is to breathe with the rhythm of life and so recognize our kinship with all forms of life. It is to appreciate every drop of water. It is to feel the warmth of the sun and to marvel at the beauty and expanse of the night sky. It is to stand in awe of who we are and where we live. It is to see the Earth with the eyes of an astronaut.

To be human is to be aware of our dependence upon the whole of the universe, and of the miracle that we are. It is to open our eyes to the simple and extraordinary beauty that is all about us. It is to live with deep respect for the sacred gift of life. It is to love.

To be human is to seek to find ourselves behind our names. It is to explore the depths and boundaries of our existence. It is to learn from those who have preceded us and to act with due concern for those who will follow us.

To be human is to plant seeds of peace and nurture them. It is to find peace and make peace. It is to help mend the web of life. It is to be a healer of the planet.

To be human is to say an unconditional No to warfare and particularly to the use of weapons of mass destruction. It is to take a firm stand against all who profit from warfare and its preparation.

To be human is not always to succeed, but it is always to learn. It is to move forward despite the obstacles.

We are all born with the potential to become human. How we choose to live will be the measure of our humanness. Civilization does not assure our civility. Nor does being born into the human species assure our humanity. We must each find our own path to becoming human.

Ruth Slickman

How to be truly human?

At sixty-nine I am still trying to learn!

Our specifically human ability to ask this question is enough to keep me wondering the rest of my days. I don't know what function we fulfill as observers and doers in this universe, but I'm incredibly grateful for the consciousness that picks up all the bits and pieces my senses collect to create this

RUTH SLICKMAN has enjoyed a long life and good health, which have given her time for several careers, including thirty-three years as a wife and mother of six children. She is now retired from the Crow Canyon Archeological Center and living in Colorado.

same ever-changing person that is *me*. For whatever reason, my participation in the whole universal process is necessary, and I know it involves being awake for the action! I believe I've been given this power of perception to experience, as deeply as possible, every element of being alive. My goal is to live every moment passionately, to rejoice humbly in the profound presence of nature, to respond appropriately to the unexpected events life presents, and to be used when I die.

Of course, in real life I'm caught up in one colossal blunder after another about two-thirds of the time. But there's no age limit on effort, so even at this date I'm trying to do what I say I want to do.

Akihisa Kondo

During the days of confusion and anxiety which affected all of Japan after the unexpectedly massive earthquake that almost completely destroyed Kobe,* depriving it of all forms of communication with the rest of the country, my mind, even though in shock, was reactivated, revitalized by the revelation that people, not used to caring very much for others in daily life, can suddenly mobilize themselves to help one another unstintingly, to brave the danger of saving lives from collapsing buildings.

AKIHISA KONDO, M.D., was a psychotherapist in Tokyo and author whose work focuses on Morita therapy, psychoanalysis, Buddhism, and the human mind.

Frankly speaking, I was becoming rather pessimistic about our human situation. After the fall of the Berlin Wall, I expected things to improve. I hoped that people would begin to realize how futile,

---

*On January 17, 1995, at 5:46 A.M. local time, Kobe experienced an earthquake of 7.2 magnitude on the Richter scale. Kobe, population 1.5 million, is Japan's sixth-largest city and the world's sixth-largest port. Seismologists identified wave phenomena during the Kobe earthquake that resembled waterside wave activity also observed in the 1985 Mexico earthquake and the 1989 San Francisco earthquake.

how tragic, it is to be driven by narrowly egoistic interests, individually, nationally, religiously. To my distress, dashing all these hopes, what followed were only atrocious wars between ethnic groups, between "races," between orthodoxies within these races. It looked as if humans were destined to keep on repeating the same follies, forever, the same self-destructive patterns, without ever learning anything from their experiences even in the very recent past. But then when this unexpected disaster of the earthquake struck, at this moment of life or death, true humanness, true human nature, asserted itself, became activated. Mutual help was given spontaneously, without anyone giving the orders. It was so encouraging; it was a relief because it was so matter-of-fact. I felt like congratulating myself, for my deep faith in the really human nature of humans had been proven, after all, to be justified.

Archbishop Desmond Tutu

God created you because God loves you. If each of us could grasp this truth and let it take root in us, there would be no place in the world for violence, for inhumanity, for ethnic animosities and genocide, for war and destruction.

DESMOND TUTU, archbishop and Nobel Prize recipient, has become a symbol of the fight against apartheid and for the dignity of African humanity.

The biblical narrative relates that, at each step of creation, God said, *"Let there be. . . ."* But at the climax, as if to signal something momentous afoot, God declares, *"Let us create man in our image and likeness."* Male and female are thus created together in the divine likeness.

This was, in fact, a remarkable assertion to make about God's human creatures and refers to a practice common in the ancient world. Since the sovereign was unable to be present simultaneously in every part of his domains, he would set up statues of himself in different parts of his kingdom. These were his *image* and *likeness*. His subjects were obliged to pay the same homage and respect to the statues as to the monarch himself. Thus for the Bible to claim that we are created in the image and likeness of God was to assert that we were God's representatives, God's viceroys.

This is a radical teaching, for it means that it is not this or that attribute (education, wealth, noble birth, membership in a particular race, etc.) that invests a person with infinite worth, but it is the fact that all are created in the image of God. It is something that is intrinsic; it comes with the package of being human. It claims for every single human person this staggering right to be God's representative, God's viceroy, God's stand-in.

The consequences are manifold. But much the most important is that people, *whatever their rank or status, whether they be poor or uneducated or whatever, should not just be respected. No, they should in fact be revered for they stand in for God.* Saint Paul teaches that we each are temples, sanctuaries of the Holy Spirit, that we are God carriers. In some of our churches you will often see a sanctuary lamp that alerts you to the fact that the Sacrament is reserved in the tabernacle and when you pass in front of it you do not just bow, but you genuflect, acknowledging the presence of God. Now if we took our theology seriously we should not just greet each other. We should really genuflect before one another. The Buddhists are more correct since they bow profoundly as they greet one another as *the God in me acknowledges the God in you.*

The worth of each individual person is intrinsic to who she is. It has nothing to do with achievement or status. But we know just how we judge people—those who fail are held to be of little account, are despised and humiliated. Our societies are often callous and treat those who are down-and-out as nonentities. It is actually blasphemous.

For the believers there is no option when faced with injustice, oppression, and racism but to oppose them with every fiber of our being. It is a religious, not a political, duty. Not to do so would be to disobey God. To treat children of God as if they were less than this is not just evil, as undoubtedly it is. It is not just painful, as it must be often for the victim of the injustices of racism and oppression. It is veritably blasphemous, for it is as if we had spit in the face of God.

We must celebrate our diversity and not claim a superiority based falsely on illusion that because we are different, therefore we are superior. *We must not allow politicians to exploit our differences and stoke the fires of tribal animosity and warfare for political advantage.* It is a dangerous game.

We must assert that God created us not for apartness, not for alienation and separation, which lead to estrangement, division, hatred, and hostility. No, God created us for family, for togetherness, for interdependence, which lead to friendliness, to sharing, to laughter, to joy, to peace, to prosperity.

As God's representatives we are meant to bear rule over the rest of God's creation, not to exploit it harshly and irresponsibly but to bear rule as God would, caringly and compassionately, not being wantonly wasteful of irreplaceable natural resources, not callously polluting the atmosphere and the rivers, but as those who are God's stewards, knowing we will have to give an account of our stewardship.

We are created "like God" to be creative in our relationships, in our work, in music, in the arts, in drama, in literature, even as gardeners. We can be creative in bringing beauty out of ugliness, peace out of war, harmony out of disharmony, order out of disorder, health out of disease. And we should not look to do what is spectacular and headline-grabbing. The mundane and unobtrusive can be equally wonderful opportunities for exercising our creativity.

We are made in the image of the glorious Trinity—we are made for family, for togetherness, for communion, for fellowship. In our African idiom we say *a person is a person through other persons*, that the solitary, totally self-sufficient person is a contradiction in terms; such a person is really subhuman. We would not know how to speak, how to think, how to walk, how to be human except we learned it all from other human beings.

We have heard it said, "Let us live simply so that others may simply live." Our faith should inspire us to work to narrow the growing gap between the destitute and the affluent, because we are members of one family, the human family, God's family. What affects part of the family will inexorably have an impact on other parts.

We are created in the image of this God who shows a marked bias in favor of the marginalized, the poor, the weak—the widow, the orphan, and the alien who usually are the weakest of the weak, the most without clout.

We are made to reach out to the transcendent. We are a remarkable paradox, the finite made for the infinite. Saint Augustine of Hippo said about God and us, "Thou hast made us for Thyself and our hearts are restless until they find their rest in Thee."

Ashis Nandy

Every age has a prototypical violence. The violence of our age is based not so much on religious fanaticism or tribal feuds as on secular, objective, dispassionate pursuit of personal and collective interests.

Every age also probably has a cutoff point when the self-awareness of the age catches up with the organizing principle of the age, when for the first time the shared public consciousness begins to own up or rediscover—often through works of art or speculative thought—what the seers or the lunatics had been saying beyond the earshot of the "sane," "normal," "rational" beings who dominate the public discourse of the time.

Thus it was the mindless bloodletting of the First World War which created a new awareness of an old psychopathology of our times. As the range of human violence and the role of science in

ASHIS NANDY is a psychologist, social theorist, and author. A leading figure in the study of human consciousness, he is director of the Centre for the Study of Developing Societies, Delhi. His books include *The Illegitimacy of Nationalism* and *The Savage Freud*.

that violence began to weigh on the social conscience, a number of European intellectuals woke up about this time to the dangerous human ability to separate ideas from feelings and to pursue ideas without being burdened by feelings. With the advantage of hindsight, one could trace the cultural sanction for this ability to changes in European cosmology in the sixteenth and seventeenth centuries. It was then that the anthropomorphic worldview began to give way to a mechanomorphic view of nature and society. It was then that what psychoanalysts may call a projective science—science heavily dependent on the psychological capacity to project into the outer world the scientist's inner feelings and pan-psychic fantasies—began to give way to a new concern with objective impersonal pictures of nature and society as the goal of knowledge and as an indicator of progress. But it was the First World War which for the first time shook the popular faith in perpetual progress through increasingly objective science.

Sigmund Freud first gave a name to the splitting of cognition and affect. He called it isolation. He described it as an ego defense, a psychological mechanism which helped the human mind to cope with unacceptable or ego-alien impulses and external threats. The event idea or the act was not forgotten; it was reincorporated into consciousness after being deprived of its affect. Freud also noted the heavy use of isolation in the character disorder called obsessive-compulsive. The connection, by itself, may not seem important, but it acquires a different meaning if we remember that some psychological works have referred to the obsessive-compulsive associations of modern authoritarianism.

Order, routine, and systems are not absolute values; an overcommitment to them could be an illness. This implies that objectivity and the separation of the observer from the observed is not an unmixed blessing; sometimes it can hide fearsome passions. Individuals isolate violent acts, including murder, from the emotions they should arouse. Societies do this on a grander scale.

George Orwell wrote:

> In our time, political speech and writing are largely the
> defense of the indefensible. Things like the continuance of
> British rule in India, the Russian purges and deportations, the
> droppings of the atom bombs on Japan, can indeed be
> defended, but only by arguments too brutal for most people
> to face . . . Thus political language has to consist largely of
> euphemism, question-begging and sheer cloudy vagueness.
> Defenseless villages are bombarded from the air, the inhabi-
> tants driven out into the countryside, the cattle machine-
> gunned, the huts set on fire with incendiary bullets: this is
> called pacification.

George Orwell wrote his essay on using English to sterilize
thinking and to cover up violence and cruelty in the mid-forties.

Erich Fromm described the authoritarian person not only as sado-
masochistic but as having a mechanical, rigid mode of thinking
characterized by isolation. Fascism, he said, thrived on the objectification of persons and groups.

Theodor Adorno and his associates, too, wrote about the "empty,
schematic, administrative fields" in the mind of the fascist and about
the constriction of his inner life. The fascist, they say, partitioned his
personality in more or less closed compartments. He had a narrow
emotional range and he rejected emotional richness, intuitions, and
the softer side of life. He admired organizations and their formal
hierarchies and he sought security in isolating hierarchical structures.

Friederich Meinecke located the origins of National Socialism in
the ancient "bipolarity extending throughout life of the Western
Man" between the utilitarian, which was stressed, and the spiritual,
which was suppressed, to the excessive emphasis on the "calculat-
ing intelligence, and to a Machiavellian rebirth which transformed
Machiavellianism from a trait of the aristocracy to that of the middle classes and, later on, to the masses."

Hannah Arendt was to later contribute to the same awareness with her portrait of Adolph Eichmann, a plain-thinking, nonideological, hardworking, bureaucratic killer who saw his genocidal responsibility as a problem of efficiency, organization, and objective planning. Arendt recognized that Eichmann was the ultimate product of the modern world, not because he established a new track record in monstrosity but because he typified the evil that grew out of everyday isolation rather than from Satanism, which comes from unbridled passions.

By the early fifties it was clear to many that fascism was a typical psychopathology of the modern world, for it merely took to logical conclusions what was central to modernity—namely, the ability to partition away human cognition and pursue this cognition unbridled by emotional or moral constraints.

Only one area of modern life escaped the full impact of the critiques of isolation: modern science. There were reasons for this. Modern science was structured isolation. The values of objectivity, rationality, value-neutrality, and intersubjectivity were definitionally the values of the modern scientific worldview. And these values did heavily draw upon the human capacity to isolate. Moreover, there was a latent awareness in the society that science was, at times, isolation at its best and its most exciting, that somehow the abstractive and generalizing capacities of science were closely related to the process of isolation.

Science as a personal search for truth and as a means of human self-realization seemed to be a form of this creative objectivity. It did not seem that isolating to many. The attacks of the artists, writers, and fashionable mystics, in contrast, were bound to wash off as eccentric responses to the creative isolation of modern science.

Implicit in such torn creative minds of this century's Europe was the belief that while the context of modern science and its applications were faulty, the text of science was liberating. In fact, as diagnosed by the modernists, the problem was that the objectivity of science had not yet fully informed the social uses of science. That is, while the scientifically minded had used isolation, they had not isolated deeply and widely enough; feelings still dominated many sectors of human life, and these sectors were waiting to be liberated by the further growth of the scientific temper to solve social problems of science by more science.

The growing body of uncritical supporters of science operate with the same folk philosophy with which, according to Bruno Bettelheim, apolitical victims often face oppression in "extreme situations." Used to being obedient to the scientific establishment, people dare not oppose the ruling ideology. Each inhumanity imposed or legitimized by science is seen as a mistake of the system which could be corrected from within it.

The idea of more science to cure the ills of science seems especially to enthuse normal scientists and the political spokesmen of the scientific estate. It suggests that while the scientific worldview cannot be judged by other worldviews, the other worldviews can be judged and indeed should be judged by science.

Which pathology has become more unsafe for human survival, that of the scientific rationality or that of its "irrational" subjects?

The earlier creativity of modern science, which came from the role of science as a mode of dissent and a means of demystification, was actually a negative role. It paradoxically depended upon the philosophical pull and the political power of traditions. Once this power collapsed due to the onslaught of modern science itself, modern science was bound to become first a rebel without a cause and then, gradually, a new orthodoxy. No authority can be more dangerous than the one which was once a rebel and does not know it is no longer so.

The moral that emerges is that modern science can no longer be an ally against authoritarianism. Today, it has an inbuilt tendency to be an ally of authoritarianism. We must now look elsewhere in society to find support for democratic values.

Ashis Nandy   277

Why has something that began as a movement of protest become part of the Establishment? Why do the moderns continue to view science as a cornered voice of dissent fighting powerful opponents when it all too visibly owns the world? Why do even the radical critics of society exercise restraint when criticizing science?

When science was primarily a philosophical venture, it allowed for more plurality. In the days of organized science there is little scope for a scientist to protect his individuality as a scientist. Overorganized science has managed to do the impossible: It has become a marketplace and a vested interest at the same time. The scientist can encase his creativity in the marketplace of science only if he plays according to the existing rules of modern science.

If a normal scientist follows that model, science rewards him handsomely; otherwise he is valued not as an eccentric professor but as a lunatic who has missed his professional bus. It is this cultural twist that has preempted basic external criticism in science.

Modern science, which began as a creative adjunct to the postmedieval world and as an alternative to modern authoritarianism, has itself acquired many of the psychological features of the latter. In fact, in its ability to legitimize a vivisectional posture toward all living beings and nonliving nature modern science is now moving toward acquiring the absolute narcissism of a new passionless Caligula.

Harvey Cox

What we need now is not a new credo but a wholly different way of thinking about what it means to be a Christian. Christianity springs from an ancient religious tradition in which the very concept of credo was unknown. Israelite faith was based on a covenant. It expressed itself through a cluster of stories, festivals, and

HARVEY COX is professor of divinity at Harvard University. He is the author of several books, including *The Secular City* and *Fire from Heaven: The Rise of Pentecostal Spirituality and the Reshaping of Religion in the Twenty-first Century.*

laws. Jesus himself never mentioned any credo. When the rich young ruler inquires of him how to enter the Kingdom, Jesus asks him what Torah requires, not what the creed states. When he meets the Samaritan woman at the well, she tries to lure him into a discussion of whether to worship "on this mountain" or in Jerusalem. Jesus rejects the theological gambit and tells her the location of worship does not matter in the least. When he calls his disciples he does not require a confessional statement but simply asks them to "follow" him. He wants them to accompany him in his work of making known and demonstrating the dawning of the new Shalom of God. Later he sends forth these same "accompany-ers" to "make disciples of all nations." The meaning of the Christian faith is for me to try to be one of these followers, a fellow traveler with Jesus and that first odd bunch of fishermen and shady characters who saw in him the start of something new.

So how did we get all bogged down with creeds? It is important to recall first of all that creeds were meant to divide, to create insiders from outsiders. They arose when some Christians began to feel that what people believed *about* Jesus was more important than just following him. Or perhaps they began to feel that in order to follow him properly one first had to believe certain things about him. But I am not persuaded that it really works that way. At the center of my faith stands not a creed but an encounter. Although it sometimes embarrasses me to talk about it, because it sounds a bit pietistic, my faith assumes the shape of a bond of trust *with* a person, not a set of propositions *about* that person.

As a theologian I have of course studied the historic creeds of the churches—the Apostles, the Nicene, the Westminster Confession, the Thirty-nine Articles, and many others. I could explain ad nauseam the cultural contexts in which they arose and why some well-meaning Christians at the time thought they were necessary. As an ecumenical Christian I have attended numerous services in which the creeds have been recited and sung. In fact, I am personally convinced that the best thing to do is to sing them, since that reminds us they are more like poetry than prose. As products of one critical stage of Christian history when our forebears in the faith struggled to come to terms with a particular culture—the Hellenistic one—they remind us of how important it is for every generation of Christians to plunge into its own cultural milieu. The question for me is not whether we "believe" this or that creed or how much of it we disbelieve or still believe or half-believe. The question is can *we* as contemporary Christians, as followers of Jesus, plunge into our postmodern, deconstructionist, religiously plural, technology-driven, global, neonationalist, Internet, Worldwide Web, postpatriarchal culture of *our* era with the same zest and imagination with which our forebears plunged into theirs?

I feel about the creeds the way I feel about the great cathedrals, paintings, liturgies, and stories of Christian history. I like being part of that history. But at the same time I know that the Crusades were preached from the ornate pulpits of those cathedrals, that *Te Deums* were sung as infidels were burned alive, and that most of what is depicted in the paintings and recounted in the stories sprang from the imagination of the artists and the balladeers. Of course I love Chartres and the Byzantine mosaics and Giotto and Dante and Michelangelo's *Pietà* and Mozart's *Requiem*. They are among the luminous landmarks in the continuing story of which I am a part. But to ask me if I "believe" any of them is to ask the wrong question. It is a category mistake. The same is true for creeds. Let's keep them, but let's remember what they are.

Now back to Jesus for a moment. The closest I get to the need for a credo is the recurrent necessity of explaining to other people (and to myself) why I still feel he is central to my life orientation and why accompanying him still makes sense to me. I fully admit that none of the explanations I come up with ever seems adequate, and I rarely find myself using the language of the historic creeds to do so (except when I sing them). I keep coming back to the realization that Jesus is central because he is a person, not an ideal or a theory or (God forbid) a theology. Consequently my relationship to him is as volatile as it is to any person. But this also makes me realize that life is about persons and that if theories or creeds get in the way, they will have to go.

Jesus anchors faith in real history. That is why—though it has its attractions—I would never make a good Hindu. I resonate with Jesus as an ultimate reference point who occasionally had sleepless nights, got angry with his coworkers, was upset when the wine ran out at the party, vexed his parents, and enjoyed the company of the riffraff of his time. I also like to believe (although there are no texts to substantiate it) that as a fully human being Jesus had to deal with the awkwardness of puberty, the shocking discovery of his own mortality, and the pleasure and messiness of relations with the opposite sex. I sometimes regret that his death at an early age prevented him from having to deal with failing eyesight, arthritis, the waning of energy, and other debilities of aging. But his thorough, *complete, and uncompromising humanness* is very important to me. I also insist that Jesus, after that midnight lynch trial, *really* died. That is why I could not be a good Muslim. They hold that it was not Jesus who died on the cross since God could and would not allow one of his true prophets (which Muslims believe Jesus was) to fall into such humiliation. But for me, humiliation and defeat are also part of life, and I like to think God has experienced his share.

I do believe that somehow or other God, or whatever you want to call the ultimate reality of the universe, feels and knows human pain and aspiration, hope and rejection. As the ecologists remind us, human life is not finally separable from other forms of life or indeed from inorganic matter. We are all made of the same stuff. But the language of the classical creeds does not help me much to explicate this interwovenness. I am sure the *"Homousia"* meant something important to people once. At least they were willing to kill each other over it. If the classical formulation was concerned with *why* God became man, I am at least as interested in what *kind* of man "God became." The gritty particularity of Jesus' humanity has become a more pressing issue for me and, I think, for our times. The real historical circumstances of his birth into a captive people in an imperial province, his constant defiance of religious and social taboos, and his resolute opposition to the Roman imperium (the great "transnational corporation" of the day) are all critical to me. The fact that the historic creeds ignore all of this (with the exception of the cryptic phrase "crucified under Pontius Pilate") demonstrates their culture-bound limitations.

I write this statement after returning from a visit to Milan, where I was the guest of the Cardinal Archbishop of that historic city,

Carlo Maria Martini, one of the most truly admirable and generous Christian leaders I have ever met. Milan is where the great Saint Ambrose was once bishop and where he baptized Saint Augustine. Today it is also a city of dazzling opulence, high fashion, and rampant worldliness. I was in Milan to speak to a huge gathering of what Cardinal Martini calls the cathedral for *believers* and *nonbelievers*. It is his own invention—an annual series of events that brings together church people and those outside the church around questions of common concern. Introducing me at the opening of the first session, Martini told them that the words *believer* and *nonbeliever* in the title of the event did not, in his view, refer to different groups of people, but to each one of us. We are all believers and nonbelievers at the same time.

I fully agree with Cardinal Martini on this. The worst thing about the creeds of the church is that they have divided us more than they have united us. They have driven out people who should have been part of the family all along, and they have included people who could talk the talk but would not walk the walk. Instead of serving as trail marks the creeds have turned into cages. Instead of poetry they have become affidavits with dotted lines at the bottom.

So let us not write any new creeds. Like the sonnet or the flying buttress, the creed is a form of human expression which once served a lofty purpose but is no longer functional. What sustains us now are a cluster of stories, a few marvelous festivals: Holy Week, Easter, and Christmas, the vision of a coming age of Shalom and delight, and—at the center—our encounter with that Stranger and Friend whose meaning we never fully grasp but whose power to attract us never fades.

Frederick Franck

FREDERICK FRANCK is the author of twenty-seven books, including the classic *Zen of Seeing.* Franck's drawings and paintings are in the permanent collections of a score of museums in the United States, Europe, and Japan. His sculptures stand in public places in the United States, Argentina, Holland, Belgium, Bosnia, and Japan. He lives with his wife, Claske, in Warwick, New York, where they restored an eighteenth-century ruin of a gristmill into an "oasis of inwardness," Pacem in Terris. In 1994 Franck was knighted by Queen Beatrix of the Netherlands.

It was only in my seventh decade that I realized that the question "What does it mean to be human?" is the vital, the central, one to which all our other questions and problems, spiritual, ethical, economic, and political, are secondary. "To be human or not be at all" is the question at this millennial shift. It first struck me when my seeing underwent a kind of mutation. "The Meaning of Life is to see," said the seventh-century sage Hui-neng.

I have been drawing—which is an intensification of seeing—all my life. A year ago or so, as I was drawing people in downtown New York—crowds and individuals in Canal Street and thereabouts—it suddenly dawned on me that what my eye perceived and what my pen was registering were not so much faces and bodies, not even "people," but life cycles, each one caught at this fleeting moment on its way from birth to death. It filled me with awe, for all at once, regardless of age and gender, each one of these disclosed itself as one—begotten, unrepeatable, at once utterly precious and pitiful.

It was not an "expansion of consciousness." It was simply its intensification, a kind of metanoia that brought me in direct touch with the Real. Each one of these life cycles had a kind of inviolate sanctity. It was not just *this* man, *that* woman, but that once-occurring life cycle.

It made me look back at my own life, now speeding to its end, and made me see the years past as a lifelong, sometimes excruciating process that led to this point at which tolerance became a bit more than that—an intense awareness of the mystery, the miracle of being here at all in Canal Street together with those others, of Existence as such. I had the feeling that at last I could be at the very least harmless to other creatures, no longer their competitor, red in claw and fang, not even their "brother," for brothers and sisters are rarely free of sibling rivalry, but somehow self-identical with all these life cycles in their infinite diversity, synchronized with them.

Schweitzer's life motto of "Reverence for Life" says in simple, contemporary words what is implied in the Gospels and the summits of Old Testament wisdom in its theistic language, that Great Compassion/Wisdom that in nontheistic terms is proclaimed by the Buddha, Lao-tzu, Chuang-tzu, Hui-neng—the answer to the question of what it means to be really, fully human, an answer that does not separate East from West but in which the twain meet, and quite intimately.

It became clear that what through the years had fascinated me in Shakespeare, touched me so deeply from Rilke's *Book of Hours*, had moved me to tears in the *Agnus Dei* of Bach's B Minor Mass, in the

Adagio of Schubert's Two-Cello Quintet in C Major, in Gregorian and Tibetan chant, was the celebration of life's fullness and its transiency, its timelessness in time. It must be the ingredient that elevates art to the status of High Art as it is manifest in Egyptian, Assyrian, and Medieval sculptures, in the sayings of Zen and Sufi masters, in Fra Angelico and Piero della Francesca, in Vermeer and in the smallest of Rembrandt's landscape drawings, in Mucho's "Persimmons" and Sesshu's angularities. But it is far from confined to High Art, for it strikes the awakened eye wherever it turns—in the glance exchanged by an old couple, in the nurse's face bent over me as I woke up from anaesthesia, in the handshake of two men on a street corner, in a child stroking a kitten—the Human.

It is precisely this ingredient of the Human that is so totally absent in the hearty voices of radio commercials, whether they speak English, French, or Japanese, in the newscasts on TV, in the deafening rock of the supermarket, the Muzak in your cardiologist's waiting room. It is not only absent, this ingredient; it is denied, mocked, by those ads for five-thousand-dollar watches, for Armani and Gucci finery, juxtaposed with, on the opposite page, the pictures of massacres in Algiers, the Congo, Bosnia, East Timor—cynical, nihilistic antithesis of the lifelong process to reach that which alone is worth knowing before the end: what it means to be fully human.

The approximately one hundred spontaneous responses that constitute this book—they are not to be the end of a chain reaction but its First Phase—justify hope and trust that humanness will yet prevail.

Editors' Note

For Frederick Franck, this image of the Human Face—nose vertical, eyes horizonal—epitomizes the Specifically Human.

He connects it with the "Original face you had before you were born" of the seventh-century Buddhist sage Hui-neng and with the "Face of faces" the fourteenth-century Christian mystic Nicholas of Cusa saw "veiled as in a riddle" in every human face.

For Franck it is the face of the other confronted as if it were his or her own.

What does it mean to be human? is the leitmotif of Franck's art and his many writings, including the classic *The Zen of Seeing*, *Fingers Pointing Toward the Sacred*, and *To Be Human Against All Odds*.